David Torkington's Trilogy
on Prayer comprises

The Hermit
The Prophet
The Mystic

The Hermit

A Personal Discovery of Prayer

DAVID TORKINGTON

ALBA·HOUSE   NEW·YORK

SOCIETY OF ST. PAUL, 2187 VICTORY BLVD., STATEN ISLAND, NEW YORK 10314

ST PAULS

Library of Congress Cataloging-in-Publication Data

Torkington, David.
    The hermit: a personal discovery of prayer / David Torkington.
        p.   cm.
    Sequels: The prophet and The mystic.
    ISBN 0-8189-0850-5
    I. Title
    PR6070.0657H47   1999
    823'.914 — dc21   98-32160
                                            CIP

Produced and designed in the United States of America by the
Fathers and Brothers of the Society of St. Paul,
2187 Victory Boulevard, Staten Island, New York 10314,
as part of their communications apostolate.

Published in the United States of America by special arrangement
with Mercier Press, Cork, Ireland.
    ISBN 0-8189-0850-5 — The Hermit
    ISBN 0-8189-0851-3 — The Prophet
    ISBN 0-8189-0852-1 — The Mystic
    ISBN 0-8189-0859-9 — 3-Volume Trilogy on Prayer

Printing Information:

Current Printing - first digit   2   3   4   5   6   7   8   9   10

Year of Current Printing - first year shown

1999   2000   2001   2002   2003   2004   2005   2006   2007

At last Saturday, the **_1_** 5th of September had come round, and I was sitting in the tiny departure lounge, waiting for the hostess to take us aboard the Island plane. I could see its small but impressive silver frame in the all too rare Glasgow sunshine.

"Would you like to take your seats, please?" The air hostess appeared like a genie out of a bottle. I didn't see her come in, but there she was in the middle of the room.

I wanted to pick up my bags and run like mad to get a good seat, but it wouldn't do for me to rush, wouldn't do for me to make an exhibition of myself. I might not be wearing my dog-collar, but I knew these Islanders; and wouldn't mind betting they knew exactly who I was, where I was going, and why! I'd probably find half of them at church in the morning. No, it wouldn't do to make a fool of myself.

The plane only seemed to hold about ten passengers as far as I can remember, or was it twelve? Anyway, we sat down on either side of the gangway.

The pilot followed us in, pleasantly smiling at everyone, and making comments about the glorious weather. He went into the cockpit, left the door open and casually began fiddling with the controls. The plane spat and hissed with annoyance, as if demanding more respect, a more serious preamble. Then he put on some flying gear, and got down to the business in earnest. Suddenly we heard his voice through the microphone; it sounded almost pompous after the initial domestic introductions.

"This is your captain speaking," said the voice, in a slightly official tone. "We are now about to leave Renfrew Airport and will be flying directly to Barra, at an altitude of about 12,000 feet. The visibility is good and I've just heard that conditions are near perfect on Barra. Please put out all cigarettes and fasten your safety belts. We're about to take off."

The plane stopped grumbling. The captain was in control now. He released the brakes and the plane taxied obediently to the end of the runway. As the lights changed to signal the "all clear," we moved off at speed.

The small plane was rattling all over. She was overdoing it, trying to show off a bit too much, but we weren't fooled. The tell-tale rattles gave her away. Even respectable middle-age had passed her by. Why on earth couldn't she be her age?

Then everything changed. We were airborne. All was calm and peaceful as we glided gently into the sky. Glasgow slouched below, gradually disappearing, as the captain pointed the proud and willing nose of the plane towards the Isles.

My mind drifted back to the various events that had led up to my journey to the Outer Hebrides.

It had all started in January. I suddenly became aware of the direction that my life was taking. To be more honest, I began to realize that it had no direction at all.

It's all rather embarrassing for a clergyman to admit that his life had become little short of being spiritually bankrupt, but I'm afraid it's the truth of the matter. The root of the problem was that I had simply stopped praying seriously. I'd all but lost the habit.

By chance I had noticed an advertisement for a weekend course on prayer at a local retreat house, so I decided to give it a go. By the Saturday night I knew that it was a flop, at least as far as I was concerned, so I was feeling a little depressed when I went into the lounge after supper. There was only one other person in the room, a quiet unassuming young woman whom I'd noticed before but never spoken to. She introduced herself as Sheila Watson.

When she asked me how I'd found the course, I tried to be as non-committal as possible at first, to find out how she felt about it.

I was quite taken aback when she said that the weekend had been a wonderful break for her, but unfortunately she hadn't got anything of any real value out of the various conferences. She explained that she was an ordinary housewife with six children, and was taking advantage of her mother's prolonged stay with the family to have a few days off. She said that it would do the family a lot of good as well as herself. The family had come to realize and accept that occasionally Mum must have a break.

Her reactions to the course were exactly the same as mine, except that I felt she was able to verbalize her misgivings far better than I could. In fact I got the distinct impression that she knew exactly what she was talking about when it came to prayer.

There was a profound sense of compassion too that simply radiated from her. It was as if she was entering into me when I began to speak. She listened with an attention I'd never experienced before. It was as if I really mattered to her, as if she really cared. No, there was no "as if" about it, she did. She wasn't just playing the role of the sympathetic listener; she wasn't just simulating the virtue of Christian love; this was the real thing, and I don't think I'd really met it before. It wasn't what she said, it was what she was.

I can't remember how it happened. All I knew was that her obvious care and concern touched something deep down within me, and I found myself telling her all about myself. She listened in rapt attention to all I had to say. It was as if I'd made a general confession with a manifestation of conscience thrown in for good measure. I'd never talked to anybody as I'd talked to her.

I suppose it was more to put me at ease than the need to share with me, that she told me something about herself, her marriage, her husband, her children, and how she had come to realize that even in a good marriage, life without prayer was meaningless to her. It was the only thing for her that made sense of everything.

I couldn't help wondering how she first started, when she first realized how important prayer was, what books she had read, and who had helped her. She admitted to me that the greatest help she'd ever received was from her spiritual director, a man of extraordinary inner depth and perception, whom she felt quite certain was a living saint. To hear someone of her spiritual caliber, talking of someone else to whom she owed everything, as a saint, simply intrigued me. I was dying to ask who he was. However, before I could ask her, she said, as if anticipating my desire, "I think you would find him of great help."

"I'm sure I would," I said, "but it is hardly practical really. What I mean is, I live in Scotland, you live in London. How can I possibly consult him, at least on a regular basis? It's all right for you, you can see him regularly, but I hardly ever get to London."

"Oh, I don't see him regularly," she said, "in fact I've never seen him at all!"

For one awful moment I thought I'd been talking to a "nut" and that she was about to tell me that the Archangel Gabriel... or one of the saints, was her spiritual director, but she quickly added, "My only contact with him is by post!

"To be quite honest with you," she went on, "I shouldn't really be telling you all this. In fact, had you not put such confidence in me this evening, I wouldn't be telling you about him now. You see my spiritual director is...," she paused for a moment and then added "now don't laugh, he's actually a hermit! I was introduced to him by a Poor Clare, who used to call at our house on the quest.

"The reason why I'm a bit chary about telling you of him is because he has actually asked his correspondents not to recommend him to anyone else, as he hasn't the time to cope with any more at the present. However, I know you really are genuine so I'll write to him for you and ask him to help."

I thanked her very much and said I would let her have my address so that she could let me know as soon as she heard from him.

"By the way, where does he live?" I asked.

"Well," she said, "it all sounds a bit too romantic to be true, but he actually lives on an Island somewhere off the West Coast of Scotland."

"Really," I said, "how interesting. I've often spent holidays in that area. Where exactly is the island?"

"Well," she said, "it's in the Outer Hebrides. It's only a small island, so small it's not even marked on the map. It's off the northeast coast of Barra."

"It's where…?" I suddenly interjected excitedly. In a flash, a picture burst into my mind of a late September evening, some five or six years ago on the Island of Barra. I knew before she went any further that I had met, or at least had seen her hermit.

"He lives on a remote uninhabited island off the northeast coast of Barra in the Outer Hebrides," she repeated slowly and hesitantly, as she saw the electrifying effect her words were having on me.

I couldn't hold myself any longer. "I've met him!" I said, bursting with excitement.

"But you couldn't," she said, "he hardly ever meets anyone."

"Well, what I mean is," I said, correcting myself, "I saw him about five years ago. I'm absolutely sure of it!"

She was looking at me dubiously, as if I was making some stupid mistake. I felt instinctively that I was right, and as it turned out, I was! I didn't pause to ask any further questions to convince myself. I was convinced, I only wanted to convince her, so I continued talking rapidly, with rising excitement.

I explained how I'd first gone to the Outer Hebrides nine years ago. I'd always wanted to go there as long as I could remember, even as a boy. I'd been fascinated by those distant islands, not for the romantic reasons that often attracted others, but because there I could pursue alone a boyhood passion that has remained with me to the present day. I was mad about birds, and like most youthful ornithologists, birds of prey were my main interest. Naturally the golden eagle was my favorite, the largest and most ferocious of all the birds of prey. I knew that several pairs of eagles nested in the Isles.

One day a local priest visiting our community casually remarked that he had just come back from his holidays in the Outer Hebrides. He was surprised to find himself bombarded with questions.

"Look," he said, "if you are so interested in the Isles, why don't you go, you can be there within an hour from Glasgow?"

There and then I made up my mind.

I got in touch with a community of nuns who ran a small hospital on South Uist, one of the larger Islands, and asked them to find me somewhere to stay for a week's holiday. They sent me the address of Mr. and Mrs. MacPherson, in Daliburgh.

I stayed with them and elsewhere in the Isles for my next five summer holidays.

Now it was on the final evening of my last stay that I was convinced I'd seen the hermit. On this particular trip I had brought a friend of mine with me, Adrian, whom I'd often promised to bring with me and introduce to the Isles.

We were staying on Barra with Miss MacClean at Ard Veenish, North Bay. After dinner we decided to go for a walk. I wanted to go down to Bruernish, to have a last look at Hellisay through the binoculars.

My interest in the island of Hellisay was not purely aesthetic. The golden eagle did, and to my knowledge still does, nest on the island, and I wanted a last look to see if I could find any trace of him.

I had seen him several times in previous years on Uist, but I had had no luck this time. I wanted to have one last look. Adrian brought the radio so we could listen to the Proms. It was a Friday evening and the London Symphony Orchestra was playing the Choral Symphony. There we sat, on the hillside above Bruernish, rapt in silence as we gazed at the beautiful scenery laid out before us and listened to the music of Beethoven's Number Nine. I think we were both overcome, intoxicated by the sheer beauty of the experience.

Adrian was staring at the various islands that surrounded Hellisay, when he nudged me, and indicated the direction he wanted me to investigate through the binoculars.

I thought for the moment he had caught sight of the eagle, but no, he was directing my attention to a small island not far from Hellisay, to which I hadn't paid much attention before. It was quite a distance away, but the binoculars were very powerful and I was quite sure I could see the figure of a man walking, or rather limping, along the coastline.

"Good Lord!" I said. "Whoever's that; what on earth is he doing out there?"

I'd always been led to believe that all those islands were uninhabited, except for a certain number of sheep that were left there to graze by some of the crofters, who lived on the mainland.

"Well, it certainly seems to be a man," Adrian agreed, "and I think he's got a limp."

"He's carrying a stick," I said, "here, you have a look." I handed the binoculars back to Adrian.

"Yes, you're right," said Adrian. "He is carrying a stick."

"Do you think he's in trouble?" I said.

"Well he certainly doesn't give you that impression," Adrian replied. Just then the man disappeared behind some boulders. We never saw him again.

When we got back to our digs, I asked Miss MacClean if she knew who the man was.

"Oh yes," she said, "he's a bit of an eccentric, a loner, who's been living on that island for getting on twenty years, though I believe he's not that old. I've seen him many a time at Mass on Sunday. He's not mad or anything, but you can't tell me he's normal, living like that for all those years."

"Is he an Islander?" I asked.

"Oh no," she said, "he's not one of us, he's a foreigner of sorts." Coming from Miss MacClean, this could mean he came from the mainland or Outer Mongolia for that matter, so I didn't pursue the point any further.

"How does he earn a living?" I said.

"I don't really know," she said, "I think he acts as a sort of shepherd for the sheep on the outlying islands, though that's hardly a full-time job. Maybe it's enough to keep him, but you wouldn't think so.

"One thing I do know," she said. "They tell me he gets an awful lot of post, and he writes a lot of letters too, to people all over the place. I believe he gets quite a number of parcels from time to time full of books, though I don't know where he puts them. He only lives in a small house that he built for himself after the fashion of a traditional 'Hebridean Black House.' Not that I've seen it myself, because it's on the easterly side of the island, so you can't see it from the mainland. If you want to know more about him, why not ask at the post office, they know more about him than I do."

I would have liked to have done that, but it was late, and I had to leave the next morning by the 11:30 plane. I had completely forgotten about the man we'd seen on that wild Hebridean island until that evening talking to Sheila in the lounge.

When I had finished my story, I could see I'd convinced my listener, who was enthralled by my tale.

"How amazing," she said. "What a coincidence!"

"It certainly is incredible," I said. "Have you ever been to the Isles yourself to see him?"

"No," she replied, "but I would love to go there. Left to myself, I would have flown out to Barra years ago, but there is an unwritten understanding between Peter and all his correspondents, that nobody should go out to visit him, and I understood this to include visiting the immediate vicinity of his chosen solitude. To my knowledge, everybody has respected his wish."

"Oh dear!" I exclaimed. "I hope becoming a correspondent doesn't mean that I won't be able to visit Barra again. I was planning a return visit next year."

"Well, you'll have to ask him yourself when you write," she said, "but I'm sure he won't be too keen on the idea."

All of a sudden the plane rolled smoothly on her side. Simultaneously we heard the voice of the captain:

"We're now just passing over Oban," he said, "if you look through the windows on the right of the plane you can see Loch Linnhe, and at the head of the loch, you'll just be able to make out Fort William… Now if you look slightly to the right, you'll be able to see Ben Nevis with a wreath of clouds around his belly. The mountains that you can see all along the horizon are the Grampians… Our present altitude is about 12,000 feet, and we are now passing over the island of Mull."

I was on the right-hand side of the plane and the panoramic view I had of the Grampians was unsurpassably superb. Although I had made this trip several times before, it was the first time I had seen anything apart from bank after bank of dirty woolen clouds.

"If you look down to the left," it was the captain again, "you will be able to see quite clearly the Island of Iona, just off the extreme southwest coast of Mull."

I didn't care what they thought of me, I wasn't going to miss this. I might never have another opportunity like this in my life. I got up, smiled profusely, and rudely leaned immediately in front of my fellow passenger, on the other side of the gangway.

I could see he wasn't particularly pleased by my ill-mannered intrusion into his "air-space," but I couldn't care less. I wanted to see Iona. I did too, very clearly indeed. I could see small groups of people milling around the church and outhouses. My unwilling bedfellow was beginning his counter-attack, by unleashing vile gravelly coughs into the side of my face. I knew the sound was artificially manufactured, to give the impression of whole battalions of pernicious germs and viruses on the rampage. I didn't want a direct confrontation so I effected a tactical withdrawal behind a battery of simulated smiles, and resumed my seat.

I later heard him talking to a man in some sort of naval uniform, in a loud affected voice. It seems he was a coastguard.

My mind wandered back to the first letter I had received from Peter. Sheila had written as she had promised giving me his address. Peter Calvay, P.O. Box 3, North Bay, Barra. She said she thought Calvay was a pen-name which he used for private reasons.

After I had received Sheila's letter, I began to realize something quite clearly, something that had been at the back of my mind ever since Sheila had told me about Peter. You see, I'd no desire to enter into a lifelong correspondence with a faceless spiritual director, however helpful he might turn out to be. For one thing, I hated writing letters of any sort, never mind long personal ones about my spiritual life. I'd known this from the beginning, though I hadn't said anything to Sheila at the time. I knew quite clearly what I wanted to do. I wanted to go to Barra to meet Peter face to face. I knew that this was the only thing that would satisfy me. I also felt that he was the genuine article. Miss MacClean was wrong, he was no oddity; not when a person of Sheila's spiritual quality could recommend him in such an uncompromising way.

I decided to write to Peter immediately. I emphasized the growing need that everybody was beginning to experience today for a deeper prayer life. I explained how inadequate I felt, and yet I was being called upon more and more to help others, when the sad fact was, I was hardly in a position to help myself! I said I fully realized his predicament, and of course it would be quite ridiculous and make life impossible for him, if everybody wanted to consult him personally. However, I went on to stress that I was in a unique position, I was an inadequate priest to whom others were looking for guidance, and how, with proper help, I would be able to put many of them on the right path. I said all sorts of other things that I can't remember now. I do remember I felt a bit of a fraud when I was sealing the letter, for overemphasizing the altruistic motives in my plea to see him, when I knew that my real motives were far more selfish.

I had to wait almost six weeks before Peter's letter arrived. It came on Wednesday, May 21st, by the lunchtime post. I picked up the letter from the dining room table where it had been left for me. The postmark was quite clear, "Barra, Hebrides." I knew that at last this was it. I dashed up to my room, closed the door like an excited, secretive schoolboy, and settled down to read it undisturbed:

P.O. Box 3,
North Bay,
Barra,
Hebrides.
May 16th

Dear Father Robertson,

Thank you for your letter. I'm afraid I haven't been too well for the last couple of weeks, so I have been unable to collect my post as usual, and when I did I had quite a backlog to get through. My schedule has been completely disrupted. It will take me some time to get myself organized again! I must say I was somewhat embarrassed by the complete confidence that you placed in me in your letter. I do hope Sheila has not been giving you the wrong impression.

To be quite frank with you, I'm only an ordinary bloke, a lay person, with a purely secondhand knowledge of the religious life and I just don't feel I have anything to offer a religious priest like yourself. I will, however, try to answer one or two points that you brought up in your letter about prayer, but I feel that, quite apart from any other considerations, it would be a waste of time and money to trek all the way out here just to see me. I will attempt to answer your long letter in more detail in a few days as I'm a bit snowed under with work at the moment and I would need more time to think about the many issues you raised in it.

Once again, my apologies for the delay. Best wishes,

Peter

I scanned through the letter very quickly the first time, interested in only one thing, did he say "Yes" or "No" to my proposed visit? As soon as I discovered the answer was no, I put the letter down. I was deeply disappointed. I had been pinning everything on going to Barra to meet Peter. The second time, I read through the letter more carefully. It said nothing to diminish my expectations of him; if anything, it increased them. Somehow the style of the letter and the tone seemed to confirm my hopes. It was a very ordinary matter-of-fact letter. No religious monograms, no pious literary exclamations, not even a religious catch-phrase to end up with. Just the non-committal "Best wishes, Peter." Funnily enough, all this impressed me rather than put me off. It had a genuine ring about it. It was a modest letter without being falsely deferential. Yes, I liked its tone. I think I'd already canonized him in my mind anyway, not just because of Sheila's introduction, or the tone of the letter, but because I desperately needed a Guru, or anyone for that matter who could help me before I gave up the struggle for spiritual survival.

There was one ray of hope, and I jumped at it. He said it would be a waste of time and money to trek out there just to see him. But what if I was going out anyway? What if I'd actually booked my holiday in Barra before his letter arrived, before I'd even heard of him from Sheila?

I knew it was a lie, but I was prepared to do anything to go and see him. But what if he was a clairvoyant? What if he could actually read your mind, he'd know I was a liar? I couldn't help but laugh at my own simplicity. I still had the rather facile idea that if I ever met a saint, he would be outwardly just an "ordinary bloke," but when nobody else was around, he'd be having ecstasies and bilocating all over the place. I couldn't help being amused by my schizophrenic image of genuine sanctity.

Anyway, I had a plan, even though it did entail an unashamed lie. I decided to do something about it immediately. I had already arranged to have my holidays in the first three weeks of September. So I rang up B.E.A. and asked them to book me a flight to Barra on Saturday, the 5th of September, and from Barra back to Glasgow the following Saturday. I thought I could attend to the other details later. I then sat down and immediately wrote to Peter.

I thanked him for his letter, and said how sorry I was to hear that he'd been ill. I explained how I had actually arranged to have my holidays in Barra even before I'd met Sheila, and that I'd arranged to stay with Miss MacClean at Ard Veenish. I then told him, quite truthfully this time, that this was my sixth visit to Barra, and how, on my last visit I'd actually seen him by accident while searching for the golden eagle, off Bruernish.

I felt sure that the true account of my previous visits to the island would counterbalance one small extension of the truth, and make it sound all the more convincing. Then came the masterstroke (or so I thought at the time). I went on to say that Father James MacDonald would probably ask me to say Mass for him on the Sunday so I would be seeing him anyway. (Miss MacClean had already said that he always came to Mass on Sunday, so I thought I'd completely wrapped him up.) He would never be able to refuse to see me now without considerable embarrassment to himself when we met.

I gleefully rushed out and posted the letter, pleased with the way I'd handled things.

Then, as usual, it happened. Later in the evening, when my emotions were subdued, my excitement lulled, I realized the enormity of what I'd done. Not only had I told a deliberate lie, but I had shamefully pulled rank, and blackmailed him into seeing me, leaving him hardly any option. I felt a complete rotter. Why, oh why do I always act so impulsively only to regret it later? I'd been guilty of an act of despicable meanness, just to get what I wanted. I didn't care a fig about the apostolate, about other people needing help. I was only thinking of myself. I was almost going to write another letter there and then, with an apology and the truth, but I thought one impulsive action would be quite enough for one day. I didn't write another letter. I let things stand, and waited in trepidation for the answer.

Peter's reply came on Wednesday morning, June 11th. I went upstairs to my room to read it alone. I had a feeling of fearful anticipation in my stomach, and although I was completely alone, my face turned quite scarlet as I opened the letter and began to read.

P.O. Box 3,
North Bay,
Barra,
Hebrides.
June 8th

Dear Father Robertson,

Thank you very much for your letter.

I didn't know that you'd been to Barra before. You seem to know the area quite well.

I mentioned you to Father James two Sundays ago. He said he remembered meeting you both here and while he was P.P. at Bornish some years ago. He said he hadn't heard from you about your proposed visit in September, but he said would you mind supplying for him during the week? It would mean saying two Masses on Sunday and one each day during the week.

He said he would leave you his car, and you could have his house to yourself for the duration.

When I saw him this Sunday, he said he'd been over to Miss MacClean at Ard Veenish to square things with her, but it appeared you'd not actually written to her as yet.

Well, Father, what can I say? You seem to have checkmated me. I can only say that I look forward to meeting you after Mass on the morning of Sunday, September 6th. If anything I can say or do will be of any value to you, I will be pleased to help, but I have a fairly tight schedule to keep to, so I hope you'll forgive me if we restrict our meetings to two hours a day between two and four in the afternoon.

I will come to you each day, if you so wish, by boat. There's a jetty at the back of the presbytery. I won't bother to bring up the points you made in your initial letter, as we will be able to discuss them at greater length in September.

Best wishes,

Peter

I didn't know what to do, what to think, or how to react. One part of me wanted to shout out triumphantly "I've done it,

I've done it!" yet another part of me wanted to squirm with the shame of how I'd done it, and at the thought of the sly way I'd trapped him.

"…checkmated me…" was the delicate and good-humored way he'd put it. Then there was the realization that he knew I'd deliberately lied to get my own way; how did he put it? "…it appeared you'd not actually written to Miss MacClean as yet.…"

He might be a hermit, but that didn't make him a fool. Of course he knew. He didn't need to be a seer to see through me!

"We have just passed over the island of Tiree." The pilot interrupted my thoughts again. I knew what he was going to say this time, but I had beaten him to it. I was already gazing down in wonder at the magnificent mountainous bulk of Rhum, rising sheer out of the sea, like an impregnable natural fortress, adorned with massive turrets over 2,000 feet high. Eigg, Canna and Muck, her island satellites, cowered deferentially at her side, content to gaze in feudal obeisance at their proud and powerful overlord. If this scene was not enough to feast my eyes upon, only half a dozen miles behind I could see the dramatic contours of the Cuillin Hills on Skye that dwarfed even the mountains of Rhum.

"I should have mentioned earlier," the captain said, "just before we approached Tiree, we flew directly over Fingal's Cave on the Isle of Staffa."

The plane changed course slightly. We were now directly facing the outer Isles. The Scottish mainland was behind us now. I settled back in my seat, closed my eyes for a moment's respite from the fierce, dazzling sunlight, and rested my senses in preparation for the next scenic orgy. I was getting more and more excited as the plane droned relentlessly on towards its destination.

Father MacDonald would be there to meet me with the car. He was catching the same plane back to Glasgow. It all worked out perfectly. He'd hand over the keys for the car and the presbytery, give me a few instructions, and we'd go our various ways until next Saturday, when we'd reverse the process. He had written to me a couple of weeks ago, finalizing the arrangements.

Once again, and for the last time we heard the captain speaking to us through the microphone:

"We are now approaching Barra. Please put out your cigarettes and fasten your safety belts." He then continued in a less official tone of voice, "I'm not sure if the sand is dry enough to land on yet, but we'll go down and have a look! If it's not, we will fly round the Isles for ten minutes, to give it time to do so!"

At that moment the plane began to lose altitude, gently stooping forward. All of a sudden the Isles seemed to be upon us. We had been aiming directly at them and before I realized it, they were on top of us.

To the right, I could see the barren, rugged coastline of Uist, trailing away into the distance. To the left I could easily make out Barra Head, the most southerly point of the Hebrides. Mingulay was just coming into view when the coastguard decided to take defensive action, as if he were anticipating a further onslaught. He picked up his morning paper and ostentatiously opened it in the middle to completely block my view.

I didn't care. There wasn't much time left and I had enough to look at out of my window. I did think of taking retaliatory action by pretending to read the front page, but I wasn't going to miss a moment of our exciting descent just to out-manoeuver him. He had obviously seen it all before. It was such a bore. Judging by the fine florid color of his face the only thing likely to excite him would be a double pink gin before lunch, or possibly two double pink gins before lunch!

My stomach suddenly lurched forward as the plane gently stuttered in her descent. Then, oh! what a view! Literally out of the blue, the plane dropped to less than a thousand feet and on the approach to the beach, she banked up, her right wing pointed to the sea. There was a hum of excitement as all the passengers looked out at the scene below. There seemed to be miles upon miles of impressive sand, the silver sands of Barra. No, it wasn't the Southern Seas, nor the Aegean, this was Barra in all her magnificence. I've seen other beaches that may claim to rival hers, but nowhere have I seen such delicate shades of color in the sea skirting the coastline: blue, emerald green and maroon predominated, but almost every shade of each merging into one another to form a kaleidoscope of pastel splendor.

Now the plane suddenly straightened and swooped down to inspect the beach. I knew that Hellisay would be visible from the other side of the plane. It couldn't have been more than a couple of miles away. However, my friend, the Rear-Admiral, had completed his blockade!

I could see the Great Cockle Beach on which we were preparing to land. We were almost upon it. I could just see a small group of people standing next to the tiny air terminal building. A couple of cars had stopped along the road to watch the landing. This was it — this was the moment the plane had been waiting for. She might be just another unimportant, undersized nobody at Glasgow airport, but here she was Queen of the Isles! Even the soaring golden eagle of Hellisay would have to stand aside as she came to inspect her dominions. You could watch the gannets dive all day into the Minch, but only once a day, and never on a Sunday, could you see this majestic sight. It was indeed a thrilling experience to watch the plane flying low over the beach, and to completely over-run the island at its narrowest, swooping up again like a huge albatross above the Atlantic.

If you could see Barra from 30,000 feet up, it would look like a large torpid turtle, languidly basking in the open sea. The body would be the main landmass, and the small head would be Eoligarry, its most northerly tip. The neck would be the narrow strip of land that joined the two together no more than four hundred yards wide, if that. On each side of this natural causeway are the two magnificent beaches, the Great Cockle Beach, facing east, where the plane would land, and the beautiful Traigh Eais. Flanked by hills and backed by a phalanx of magnificent sand dunes, the Traigh Eais has no equal in the Isles.

Apparently the sand had sufficiently dried out, and, greatly to my disappointment, the plane was preparing to make her landing. Reaching the top of her imperious swoop over the sea, she banked up, this time to the left, affording new and enchanting views to the passengers as she turned to make the most of her final entrance, with all the haughty dignity she could summon.

The journey was over. She landed and taxied over to the air terminal where Father James was waiting to meet me. We sat down in the sultry heat of his small mini-estate, while he went over the practical details of where I would find everything, and what had to be done. He said he had arranged for Mrs. MacNeil to come in and "do" for me. Peter would, as usual, come in for lunch after the eleven o'clock Mass on Sunday.

I thanked him for everything, picked up my bags that had been brought to the car directly from the plane, and drove off to North Bay. It was scarcely two miles away. When I arrived at the presbytery, I found Mrs. MacNeil waiting for me, to show me my room and where everything was.

I didn't do much after lunch. I just wandered over to Ard Veenish to see Miss MacClean and cadge a cup of tea. I didn't go out in the evening, I suddenly felt tired. It had been a tiring day, certainly one of the most unforgettable days in the whole of my life! Almost the perfect day. Could it be the beginning of the perfect week?

2

I woke up feeling warm and well rested; a sense of deep contentment welled up within me, and extended to every part of my being. I yawned like a big, fat contented cat and aimlessly rolled out of bed to see what the morning had to offer. Pleasant soothing memories of the previous day had lingered on through the night and still remained with me as I opened the curtains, to be greeted by a dull doleful day. Heavy dark clouds seemed to cling round everything in sight. The clammy, Hebridean mist scarcely disguised a gentle, but relentless drizzle, that made even the stones look soggy. I felt like drawing the curtains on this scene of misery and heading back to bed, but things had to be done. Practical things had to be attended to. There were doors to be opened, cupboards to be unlocked, and the various vestments and vessels to be prepared for the altar. I quickly washed, shaved and got down to work.

Several people appeared out of the mist at about a quarter to eight, and by the hour, the church was more than half full. I didn't preach for long. I felt it would hardly be appreciated by a bedraggled congregation, who had already suffered enough at the hands of the hard and heedless elements.

I'd dug out an old sermon, as I usually did on such occasions. After all, I was on holiday and in any case, I wanted to use a well-tried one that I thought would go down well in front of Peter. The first Mass was the "dress rehearsal."

I called the sermon "God the Plumber." Originally the idea had come from Bonhoeffer's *Letters,* especially the one dealing with

"Religionless Christianity." The "God of the Gaps" became "God the Plumber" — the man we called in when something goes wrong, but whom we forget about when all is running smoothly!

Now it was after Mass, after breakfast in fact, that things began to happen; things inside me, I mean. It was about 9:45 a.m. when I started to get that strange "scared feeling" in the pit of my stomach. Until that moment, it had been all "go." I'd hardly had time to think since Thursday night. In an hour I would meet Peter for the first time, and I felt as if I were waiting to go into my oral finals all over again. I even began to shiver with fearful anticipation, so I put on the fire. I know it all sounds ridiculous, but I couldn't help it. All the pushing, all the skulduggery to get him to meet me, and now the time had come, I was scared. It's easy to connive, to lie, to scheme your way into someone's privacy from the cozy security of your own room, several hundred miles away, but when it comes to meeting them face to face on their own ground, it is quite a different matter.

I spent most of the time before the eleven o'clock Mass, thinking of the various ways I should react to Peter when we actually met. I started the Mass in a state of nervous tension that I had not experienced for years. I believed that Peter would be somewhere in the congregation watching me at that moment.

I had regained sufficient control of myself by the time I began the sermon, to briefly scan through the congregation to see if I could spy anyone who could possibly be Peter. It was then that I suddenly stopped in my tracks.

I forgot completely what I was trying to say for a full thirty seconds. And that's quite a long time — a terrifyingly long time if you happen to be the preacher. I had been knocked hopelessly off balance by a man who was staring at me defiantly, from the end seat in the front row. A tall, well-groomed, ruddy-faced man, a man I'd thought could only be excited by the prospect of a double pink gin — it was my old "friend," the Rear-Admiral! I don't know who was the more surprised. He had the advantage over me —

he'd had a good eight and a half minutes during the readings to get used to the idea of who I was.

Why on earth couldn't he have gone to the back of the church or have sat in an inconspicuous seat instead of sitting staring at me from the front seat; surely he should have known the effect it would have on me when our eyes would inevitably meet? Even that inevitability could have been avoided if he'd only had the decency to lower his eyes, instead of staring at me like that!

It took me two minutes to gain some sort of composure again, after a fearful pause, a couple of stuttering restarts, and innumerable contrived coughs.

It was fortunate that I had chosen to use an old, well-worn sermon that I knew backwards. If it had been a new one, or if I had tried to make a few extempore remarks about the Gospel as I sometimes did, it would have resulted in a humiliating disaster.

I was able to regain my composure by referring all my remarks to the left-hand side of the congregation, so as to avoid any further eye-contact.

It was then that it happened. It happened so quickly that I hardly saw anything clearly definable. It started with a click. It was the click of the sacristy door opening. Several heads turned to the right, as a silent figure came out of the sacristy, to take up a position in the side aisle. I didn't see the man properly, but I knew who he was. I saw the stick, I noticed the limp, hardly noticeable, but I instinctively knew that I hadn't made a mistake.

That was enough for my nerves for one day. Enough was enough, and I'd had enough!

I don't know to this day where I was up to in the sermon. I just said something like: "...and so we should think of God, not on the outside, as it were, but at the very center of the human predicament."

And that was that! I can't remember what happened then, the rest of the Mass remains a blur in my memory. As soon as I'd got my vestments off at the end of Mass, I hurried round to the back of the church to meet the people — not that I was in the mood to meet them, especially after that sermon!

I couldn't decide how to react to Peter when we met, so I decided to keep on doing things, keep dashing about until he came to me. Then I'd look dazed and vague, as if I'd forgotten he even existed. I would then warmly shake him by the hand, like a long-lost brother who'd just turned up out of nowhere.

I reached the back of the church to see the Rear-Admiral backing his car out of the forecourt and driving off in the direction of Castlebay. He saw me, even glared at me, but gave no sign, no signal of recognition. He drove off into the mist and out of my life forever. I could imagine him making straight for his desk to write a letter of invective to the Catholic Press about those "polo-necked priests" who were a disgrace to the Church.

I was interrupted from my uncharitable, but regular habit of mentally pigeon-holing people, by one of the parishioners who told me I was wanted on the telephone.

"Oh, by the way, Father," said the man, "would you please tell Peter I've put his things in the boat, and you can tell him from me, I never thought he'd become a gentleman of leisure."

"OK!" I shouted as I rushed into the house. It was the neighboring parish priest who kindly invited me over for dinner that evening.

I put the phone down, walked into the dining room, and there he was, sitting next to the table. He got up as I came in, smiling naturally as he took me by the hand. I was almost instantaneously brought to the floor. For a moment I thought he intentionally meant to do me an injury.

"I'm terribly sorry!" he said, immediately releasing his frightening grip. He had genuinely hurt me. I sat down nursing my hand, to the accompaniment of his profuse apologies. He had hurt me all right, but I made the most of it. Things couldn't have turned out better.

The moment we'd met, the psychological advantage had gone to me. Instead of me feeling guilty and trying implicitly to apologize to him for what I had done, he was the one who was apologizing to me!

"It's all right," I said, bravely forcing a smile.

"I just forget about these hands of mine," he said, as if he'd only had them for a few weeks. "I've always been in trouble with them ever since I was a teenager. You see, I have to depend on my hands so much because of my leg. I have to grip things more firmly than anybody else for security. My father was endlessly telling me off at home because I would casually turn the taps off in the bathroom and go out for the evening, and nobody could turn them on again!" He laughed guiltily, as if he were anticipating another scolding.

The words "father," "home," "teenager," broke the spell I had cast round him. So far he had been little more than a stereotype stamped out in my mind. All of a sudden he had come alive. He was a person; an individual with a past, a mum and a dad, a home, and a history. He had a face too and a body — a big body! He was a well-made man, about five foot eleven, with strong, powerful shoulders, supporting a heavy, well-shaped head with a mop of black hair, not shoulder length, but long enough to cover both his ears.

The man I was expecting to meet would have been at least fifteen years older. Peter looked in his late thirties, or possibly forty, but even my arithmetic told me he must be at least forty-two. I would say he had worn well, in spite of the "tell-tale" grey hairs, that were by no means abundant. A handsome man, no doubt about that. This was something I'd not expected either. It was a strong face with a touch of stubbornness about the chin, but the face had been softened through suffering, and was mobile with compassion. He wore a large donkey jacket, heavily patched with genuine leather at the elbows. Perhaps it was the thick white Aran sweater underneath that gave him such a heavy, powerful appearance. His trousers were strong black "cords," and his right foot was supported by a large, built-up boot, fitted to an iron caliper, and oddly enough, he was wearing a massive home-made sandal on the other.

"Are you all right?" he insisted, with genuine concern.

"Yes, yes, I'm fine, thanks, though I wasn't expecting to meet an 'all-in wrestler,'" I said, attempting to be funny. "Well now," I said, trying to take control of the situation and play the host, "would you like a drink before dinner?"

"If you don't mind, Father," he said, breaking out into another guilty smile, "I'd prefer to have a bath. Father James usually lets me have one each Sunday before dinner, so I've just got time if I go now."

"By all means," I said. "We'll meet in half an hour for dinner, if that gives you enough time?"

"Plenty, thanks," he said. "It won't take me long." He picked up an old sports bag, took his stick that had been hanging over the back of the chair, and went upstairs.

I sat down with a sigh of relief. The worst was over; the introductions were done. Thanks to his incredible physical strength and to no skill of mine, all had gone well.

A gong sounded at one o'clock. Peter arrived punctually with Mrs. MacNeil's soup, and the meal began.

It wasn't a pose but he didn't help too much to push the conversation along, at least not to begin with. Silence didn't seem to embarrass him as it did me, but after all he was hardly accustomed to indulge in trivial table talk. After he'd asked me about my journey, and I'd enthused about the glorious trip I'd had on the plane, it was I who felt under pressure to keep the conversation going.

When the meal was over, we sat down in front of the fire.

"I notice you've got a northern accent," I said, wondering how he would react. It wasn't very broad, but it was quite evident that he'd made no attempt to soften it down, or cover it up.

He smiled readily. "They'd hardly call Manchester north up here," he answered pleasantly.

"Were you brought up in Manchester?" I asked.

"Yes," said Peter, showing no unwillingness to talk about his past. Why should he?

I had made up my mind not to pry, but after all, this wasn't prying. I was only asking perfectly normal and natural questions about his past. I'd have done the same with anyone else.

"I expect you went to school there?" I said to him.

"Yes, that's right. I went to St. Bede's College."

"Really?" I said, "I've been there myself. I gave a retreat to the nuns who look after the boys. They're the Franciscan Missionaries of St. Joseph, I think."

"Yes, that's right," said Peter. "One of the Sisters whom I actually remember from school writes to me now."

"What did you do when you left school?" I asked. The tone of voice betrayed me. I realized it too late. It was quite obvious that I was bluntly probing for information. However, without any hesitation, or giving any sign of reluctance, he readily volunteered to continue.

"I went to teacher training college in London," he said, "St. Mary's, Strawberry Hill, taking French and Geography as my main subjects. When I'd finished there, I went to the Sorbonne in Paris. When I'd finished my studies I taught for two years in London, and then I came out here."

Though he spoke quite naturally and factually about his past, I was later to find out, from a priest in the Salford Diocese, far more about his school days. He was universally remembered and loved as a boy. Head of the school, cricket captain, rugby secretary, star of plays and operettas, and an active member of innumerable school societies. He seemed to be involved in almost everything in some capacity, in spite of his leg (the result of polio which he caught when he was six). Naturally he couldn't play rugby, but I was told that his powerful bass voice scored more tries for the school than any wing three-quarter. Though deprived of playing rugby he could play cricket and with the help of a runner, he was a formidable batsman. Boys in the playground would moan when he got hold of the bat because nobody could get him out!

In spite of my resolution not to pry, his readily available answers gave me confidence, and I couldn't help coming back for more.

"Do you mean you dropped teaching just like that, and came out here?"

"Well, it wasn't quite as simple as that," he admitted, preparing to tell me more. "You see while I was a student I had a crush on Thomas Merton. I read *Seven Storey Mountain*, and after that I couldn't stop. I read everything of his that I could lay my hands on. I was terribly impressed by all he wrote; his writings touched something deep down in me. I felt compulsively attracted to the life and ideals he stood for. I used to go to Mount St. Bernard's and stay there for weekends. I even stayed at Citeaux while I was studying in Paris.

"It was while I was still at St. Mary's, Strawberry Hill, that I asked to be admitted as a Cistercian novice at Mount St. Bernard's. The novice master was a little wary of prospective novices at that time. 'That man Merton will be the death of me,' he said. In the year I applied, they had had two hundred applications to join them, most of which were put down to the severe epidemic of 'Mertonitis,' that was rampant in the early to mid-fifties. Out of two hundred, they only accepted six. After an agonizing wait, I was finally accepted, but told to finish my studies and do a year's teaching before entering. I was overjoyed. I had always wanted to become a priest, but never seriously applied before because of my leg. That didn't seem to be even considered as a problem at Mount St. Bernard's.

"It was during my first year's teaching that I began to have second thoughts about the Cistercian way of life. I remember one Saturday going down to Cowfold to visit the Carthusians, but that didn't seem to be what I was looking for either. I wanted to give myself radically to God, as a contemplative, but gradually I began to realize that neither the Cistercians nor the Carthusians were for me.

"Then during my first year's teaching I got friendly with another young teacher who came from South Uist, and I stayed with him for a month's holiday in the summer. He lived near Daliburgh, almost opposite the hospital. The local headmaster asked me to teach there for a year. I enjoyed it very much, but when at the end of that year I was offered a teaching post in America, I realized I had to make a decision. I decided to take a year off and do a year's retreat on the Island of Vatersay (the least inhabited island in the Hebrides). I stayed there for four years!

"After that I decided I would like to continue, as a layman, giving my life to God, against the background of a simple Hebridean life. I was offered a job as a part-time shepherd on Barra, looking after the sheep that were left to graze on the small islands off Bruernish. I couldn't resist the greater solitude that was offered to me by making my home on the small uninhabited island of Calvay."

So that's why he calls himself Calvay, I thought, Sheila was right. It was a pen-name.

"I could barely keep myself as a shepherd," he continued, "so I did a little painting and a bit of fishing and now I find I can get by.

"It's only in the last few years that people started calling me a hermit. I can't help but be amused by the title, though it can be highly embarrassing on occasions, especially when people like you come all the way out here to see me, as if I were a latter-day John the Baptist!"

I colored slightly, but didn't say anything.

"I suppose I've got Sr. Veronica to blame," he smiled, good-humoredly.

"Sr. Veronica. Who's she?" I said.

"Oh, she's a nun who came from Bruernish originally. We used to have long talks about prayer. She started everything by recommending me to her friends and so the letters began. If I'm not careful, I'll have to open a correspondence school on Calvay with a couple of secretaries!" He laughed without any bitterness, but in vague, bewildered amusement at what had happened over the last few years.

I hadn't interrupted him while he spoke about the main steps that had led to his setting up home on Calvay, but I'd been absolutely fascinated throughout. It was not so much what he said, though that was interesting enough in itself, but for a variety of reasons I find difficult to express.

First, I had misread him completely. This was my own fault — I was forever building up people's characters on too little evidence.

I had just assumed that Peter would be so jealous about his privacy, his past, his way of life and his solitude, that he would have placed "No Entry" signs everywhere about his person. "Private — Keep Out" would be printed large upon his forehead. But that wasn't the case. He certainly wasn't garrulous, nobody could accuse him of that, but you got the distinct impression that he was completely transparent, had no secrets at all, and was prepared to talk in a simple, unaffected way about himself, or anything else for that matter.

Every time I asked a question, I was looking for the warning signs, watching his eyes, looking for the slight muscular movements of the face that would tell me I was approaching dangerous ground, but I never observed any at all. There was a soft innocent simplicity about him that made me feel I could ask him questions of the most personal and delicate sort, and he would answer without hesitation and without any trace of irritation whatsoever.

Everybody has a point where they draw the line, when they say enough is enough, and "Verboten" bars the way. I knew I hadn't really pressed him, but I could see quite clearly that he didn't know the meaning of the word "Verboten" when it came to encroaching upon his privacy.

Then there was something else about him, that I might not have noticed had I not been unnecessarily worked up into a state of ridiculous hypertension at the prospect of meeting him. There was a hardly definable "something" about him that gently exuded tranquillity and peace.

When he had finished talking to me I was completely restored to my normal self again. I was relaxed, completely at ease and restored to a state of equilibrium.

Having said all this, however, I think it is only right to point out that this first meeting with Peter was by no means as striking as my encounter with Sheila. The impact of my first meeting with her was hardly less than traumatic, for a variety of reasons that I have never fully been able to understand.

It was different with Peter. You couldn't help but like his totally unaffected and natural disposition, his transparent honesty and irresistible simplicity, but having said this, I have said all I can to convey my first impressions accurately.

"Well," said Peter, suddenly looking hard at his watch, "I must go now, Father. I have several things to do before night fall, so if you'll excuse me…?"

"Certainly," I said, as we got up simultaneously, and walked out of the dining room into the hall.

"Oh, by the way," I said, "one of the parishioners said he'd put your gear in the boat."

"Oh, I'm pleased," he said. "That'll save me a trip to the post office. It'll be my weekly provisions and the post."

"And he said something about 'he never thought you'd become a gentleman of leisure,'" I interjected, looking somewhat puzzled.

"Oh," he said, "he was referring to the boat. Father James has left me his outboard motor for the week to save me all that extra rowing. That's why I'm afraid I was late for Mass. I couldn't get the confounded thing started." He jerked his head upwards and pulled a face that indicated he disclaimed all responsibility for the vagaries of a modern mechanical motor — far less dependable than a pair of good strong hands.

"I'll see you tomorrow then, Father," he said. "At about two o'clock, if that's all right?"

"That'll be fine," I said. "I'll look forward to seeing you then."

He picked up his sports bag and, with the aid of his sturdy stick, made his way down to the path, towards the jetty.

I came in, shut the door, and sat down in an easy chair to relax and to ponder quietly over the strange and various happenings of that eventful day.

29

I began to feel disappointed, even depressed. The scales that had been obscuring my vision for the last six months were gradually beginning to fall from my eyes, and I was able to see more clearly, more accurately. What I began to see, what I began to realize, was that my little dream had come to an end.

Like a child, I'd created a fantasy world in my imagination, of a wizard on a magic island, who would make all my dreams come true. But what had happened when I had come face to face with the "wizard" who was supposed to wave his wand and turn the beast into a handsome Prince Charming?

I had been confronted by a simple, good man, who once had aspirations to become a monk, but who was now, as he said himself, merely trying to live a decent Christian life, "Far from the Madding Crowd."

I had no doubt about his sincerity, or his honest-to-God Christian piety and goodness; that was obvious. He hadn't tried to deceive me, or anyone else for that matter. He had made his position plain before I came to the Isles.

He was of course quite right. How could he possibly understand or appreciate the pressures, the tensions and anxieties of a contemporary religious from the remote halcyon seclusion of his island retreat? How could a man who had separated himself so completely from the modern world, possibly have any idea of the psychological strain and inner conflicts of faith, that the modern world placed on a young priest?

My need was so great, my desire for help so acute, that I refused to hear the first piece of common-sense advice that he had given me. A piece of advice that would have saved so much trouble and embarrassment for the two of us; if I'd only listened!

Once again, it all seemed to add up to one thing. I'd made a fool of myself. That stupid emotional and impulsive flaw in my personality had let me down again. Why, oh why, did God make me such a blind, romantic dreamer?

I began to laugh quietly to myself, shaking my head in a gesture of despair at my own incorrigible stupidity. At least I could laugh at myself — that was something! At least I could laugh at the ridiculous position I had put myself into this time.

I'd ended up once again, in another "cul-de-sac." This time in one of the remotest places in Britain!

It was another dead-end; or so I thought. But thank God, I had made another mistake, misread another situation and failed completely to recognize the quality and depth of the man I had just met.

I'd met the man who was going to change my life completely, a man who would speak to me of the intimate details of the spiritual life, with a precision and profundity that I'd never yet encountered, and probably never would again.

This man, I was soon to learn, was a mystic, in the literal and fullest sense of the word. His knowledge was the knowledge that only comes from experience.

This was why, when he began to speak about prayer and the spiritual life, he would speak with a confidence and conviction that would leave me in no doubt at all, that here indeed was "…a man who spoke with Authority."

3

Peter had failed to live up to my puerile expectations and, while I had no objections to meeting him again, as I would be doing that very afternoon, I could no longer see the point, or the desirability of spending two hours a day talking to him about topics of importance to me, which would of necessity be outside the range of his experience, and hence, his understanding.

I began to think up excuses to present to him, as a pretext to reduce our future meetings to two. This would give me at least two full days to visit friends on Eriskay and South Uist.

I was pleased for Peter's sake that the weather had called a temporary truce to the fierce assault it had inflicted upon us the previous day. The mist had not dispersed, but had retreated to the nearest high ground where it gently but nonetheless effectively beheaded every hill that dared to rise above a hundred feet!

I can't remember how the conversation got under way. I'd made up my mind that Peter would not be able to help me in any appreciable way, so I'd decided to keep my distance.

I didn't want to appear pompous, or play the role of the cocky interviewer, but I thought I could do worse than adopt the "gentle probing question technique" I'd used so successfully the previous day. I wanted to avoid appearing rude, however, or embarrassing him, so I started by hiding my opening gambit behind a smoke-screen of vague generalizations about the spiritual poverty of the contemporary world. Then I made my move.

"What do you think is the recipe for escaping from the moral morass that we've all got ourselves into?" I said, feigning bewilderment.

"Love," Peter answered.

"Yes, if only we would love one another consistently," I said, simulating sincerity. (One good cliché deserves another, I thought!)

"Oh, I'm not talking about our love," he said, with a sudden directness that took me by surprise, "I'm talking about God's.

"I believe the distinction is very important and not purely academic. If you'll bear with me, I'll explain what I mean." Peter was looking both relaxed and alert at the same time.

"I had a cousin called John," he said, "who was a bit of a rake." He wasn't smiling. He pursed his lips together, slightly nodding his head, as if the memory of the incident he was about to relate still brought back painful memories into his mind. "If he wasn't genially propping up the bar at the rugby club, he was engaged in a similar exercise at the golf club. He drank too much, smoked incessantly and generally ended up late at night gambling. Even though he was quite well off, he soon got into debt.

"His mother didn't see him for days on end. She had no idea where he slept, or whom he slept with for that matter. The rest of the family were more concerned for my aunt than for my cousin. He seemed to thrive on his revelry, as if the physical effects of his life-style 'by-passed' him and were inflicted by some ugly twist of fate on his mother instead. It was a sort of 'Dorian Gray' situation, where his mother took the place of his own decaying portrait. Everybody in the family had rows with him. There were frightful scenes, endless flare-ups, and he even came to blows with an uncle of mine on one occasion. I tried with the rest of them, but got nowhere.

"We had all given up, when things dramatically changed, or so my aunt said. It was almost as if he had had a conversion experience, been struck by an angel of light, or something heavy! My aunt didn't know what to make of it at first, couldn't for the life of her find out what had happened. Then after a few weeks he arrived home with a tiny Korean nurse called Nina, whom he'd met at a party. She was nothing to look at, quite plain in fact, but he was hopelessly in love with her and they had already decided to get married. In normal circumstances my aunt would have raised all sorts of objections, rational and irrational, but she was so overjoyed at the change that had come over her son, so grateful to the girl for what she had done, that she readily agreed.

"He was a changed man. At the time I was convinced that he was already an alcoholic. I thought his case was hopeless. One thing I'm sure of to this day is that he'd never have changed his lifestyle on his own; he couldn't. Things had got out of hand, gone too far. Not only did he stop drinking and gambling, he also stopped smoking. He had to pay off his debts and then start saving for a mortgage.

"Rows, arguments, quarrels, couldn't change him, neither could warnings or threats. Reason, appealing to his better nature, pleading for consideration for his mother, were a waste of time and got nowhere. In the end only one thing got through: love. The love of this four-foot-eight, seven-and-a-half-stone Korean nurse, Nina! It's twenty-four years since all this happened; next year will be their twenty-fifth wedding anniversary."

Peter paused, aimlessly staring into space for a moment.

"I hope I've not been boring you with my reminiscences," he said.

"Not at all," I said genuinely. He had spoken colorfully with a fluency that made him easy to listen to. I was pleasantly surprised. He was a natural raconteur, though oblivious of his ability to captivate his listener.

"That incident has had a deep and lasting effect on me," said Peter, pulling himself together.

"I was fascinated by the tremendous power of love in action. No power on earth could have done anything for my cousin. It helped me to realize that if we could somehow place ourselves in the way of God's love, put ourselves under the influence of His creative power, then like John, we might be radically and permanently changed; not superficially, but from our innermost parts.

"When I began to read the New Testament in earnest, I saw that this is what it's saying time and time again. I was staggered to realize that I'd never noticed it before. I'd missed the wood for the trees. I'd missed the whole point of the Gospel. Everything suddenly began to make sense, the pieces of the jig-saw started to fall into place once I'd discovered the central piece.

"The story of Jesus is a unique and world-shaking example of what happens to a man who dares to expose Himself totally to God's love. It is the story of how Jesus was possessed by the love of God, and the effect that this had on His life and on the lives of others. Invaded by love of this force and magnitude, Jesus was enabled not only to listen to people and care for them, but to enter into them, heal and cure them, restore them to wholeness and even raise them from the dead; for there's nothing that can resist the power of uncreated love, not even death."

Peter leaned forward on the edge of his seat, his shoulders slightly hunched, his right elbow resting on the arm of the easy chair.

"The more I tried to steep myself in the Scriptures, in the writings of the Fathers of the Church, in the most ancient and hallowed traditions of Christian spirituality, the more clearly I came to see that the message was always the same. The burning question was not firstly 'how do we love God?' but 'how do we welcome God's love into our lives? How do we best position ourselves to be the recipients of that love?' Once we get this right, everything else falls into place, as it did for John.

"The trouble is, we've presented Jesus as a sort of celestial super-salesman who has come to sell us the latest up-to-datest encyclopedia of moral behavior, in the mistaken belief that if you can present it to people in a convincing enough way, they won't be able to resist it! But He didn't come primarily to detail the way we ought to love God and our neighbor; He came to give us the power to do it. Without the power to do it, we can read the Bible till we are blue in the face and say 'how beautiful, how uplifting,' but no moral code however well reasoned, however lofty, however sublime will ever permanently change a person. But love can! God's love certainly will if it is only given a chance."

He had made his point. He closed his mouth tightly, leaned back in the easy chair, joined his huge hands, palms facing the floor, and unceremoniously cracked all his fingers together.

"I think the majority of people would agree with you," I said in a rather hurried tone of voice, as if I wanted to go on to more important matters. "But most people are asking more practical questions."

Peter smiled, almost laughed.

"I know most people would agree with me in theory," he said, "but in practice most people act quite differently. Nine out of ten Christians, no, forty-nine out of fifty," he corrected, "are in practice Pelagians."

"Semi-Pelagians you mean, don't you?" I said. I could have bitten my tongue off the moment the words were out of my mouth.

"Sorry… Semi-Pelagians," said Peter, quite unconcerned, even grateful for my intervention.

"What I mean to say is," said Peter, anxious to clarify his meaning, "we think we can change ourselves and direct the course of our spiritual growth by dint of sheer muscle-power and dogged endurance, but we can't. The trouble is we've been brought up with a completely one-sided view of heroism.

"In storybooks, adventure novels, in every variety of fiction and even in true-life stories, the hero and heroine are always presented in the same way. They are the lonely intrepid pioneers, explorers or adventurers, who dream dreams, have visions and by taking themselves by the scruff of the neck, squeeze out every reserve of energy that they possess to make their dreams come true, and transform their visions into reality.

"They inevitably tend to be rather remote figures, loners, aloof, independent, self-contained. They are the archetypal self-made men. They are not born great, they do not have greatness thrust upon them, they achieve it by themselves, by setting their wills in iron, 'straight-jacketing' their bodies with self-discipline and by refusing to look right or left, or anywhere that will distract them from their single-minded purpose.

"This may work in paperbacks, it might sometimes work in real life, but it will never work in the spiritual life. There is no such thing as a do-it-yourself spirituality. But no matter what you say or how many times you say it, we've all been tarred with the same brush. We all think that we can do it ourselves.

"A person normally begins by enthusiastically mustering their inner resources, 'setting their teeth hard, spreading their nostrils wide' as they endeavor to take themselves in hand. It doesn't matter how hard they try, how optimistically they flex their mental muscles or clench their fists, failure is only a matter of time. In this enterprise, the 'tough guy' approach inevitably leads to failure.

"The exceptionally stubborn might push things to the limit before they finally crack up in a fit of depression, self-pity and despair, but the majority settle for a compromise. They sense failure before it comes and tactfully avoid the humiliation of facing their own weakness by lowering their ideals and putting off until tomorrow the steps they feel are necessary to attain them. They reassure their guilty consciences with dreams of tomorrow's fresh start, when they will begin again in earnest to take themselves in hand and get down to the serious business of pulling themselves together."

It is strange how even unpleasant truths about oneself are amusing when they have a sharp edge and are delivered unwittingly and without malice. I think the element of surprise is important to have the desired effect. It's rather like suddenly being confronted by your own face caught in an affected pose in a shop window, or an unexpected and insolent mirror that refuses to lie and brazenly presents you to yourself exactly as you are. If such a sight fails to amuse then you're blind and more than half dead.

I couldn't help but smile.

"You're smiling," Peter said, slightly surprised by my reaction.

"I'm really laughing at myself," I said, hastening to reassure him. "What you were saying suddenly triggered off something in my memory. I was thinking about my novitiate days," I said, laughing openly as the memories came into focus in my mind with humiliating clarity.

I remembered how, towards the end of my first month, I decided I ought to become a saint. After all, I thought, that's why I'd come. In a truly professional way I set about it, drawing up the blue-prints, planning a strategy. Not wishing to be too ambitious, I thought I'd go slowly and do the job thoroughly, so I generously allowed myself a whole year to complete the process of my sanctification! The completion of this laudable enterprise was timed to coincide with my parents' visit, at the end of the year, for my Simple Profession. They would come, innocently unaware that their erstwhile and errant offspring was no more. The familiar shape and form were merely the cast for the new-mold man within!

The plan was to acquire a different virtue each month. I remember dividing the most important virtues into eleven and deciding to devote a month to the mastery of each. I actually wrote the name of the chosen virtue under the title of each month on my calendar. I tacitly agreed with myself that even if I completely mastered a virtue by the middle of the month I wouldn't presumptuously move on to the next, but would humbly spend the last couple of weeks meekly practicing what I had acquired. I started with Humility because the book I was reading said it was the foundation of all the other virtues. November was set aside for Obedience. December for Charity and so on.

Unfortunately I'd slightly miscalculated and I didn't quite manage to finish, in fact I've never quite managed to finish! I did try to continue my efforts, even to redouble them in my first year as a student, but none too soon I realized that "discretion is the better part of valor" and I reluctantly lowered my sights, partly blaming my studies, and promised myself a new beginning in the near future. I have been faithful to that promise ever since and renew it regularly, at least twice a fortnight!

Peter laughed readily when I explained to him the spiritual gymnastics of my first fervor. He told me how, when he was at school, he had written to a Carmelite to ask if he could purchase a hair shirt. The friar had written back to explain that he would be delighted to accede to his commendable request, but, according to ancient monastic tradition, hair shirts were always woven from the full head of hair of the wearer, hence the tonsure, so would he please forward his scalp by return of post.

We both laughed at the Carmelite's sense of humor. Peter plainly enjoyed a joke and wasn't ashamed to laugh loudest of all at his own.

"But do you see what I mean?" Peter interjected as our laughter died down. He was in earnest again.

"We all thought we could do it ourselves; people still do. Though I don't suppose the modern 'do-it-yourself-kit' is the same as ours."

"But what else could we have done at the time?" I said, as if the intervening years had taught us both quite clearly what we ought to have done.

The intervening years may well have been a school of wisdom for Peter, but I'd still not learned my lessons; I was only beginning to see my mistakes, so I added after a brief pause:

"What else can we do?"

"Well," said Peter. "The only thing we can do is to swallow our pride and accept the truth that stands out like a sore thumb; namely that we can't do anything by ourselves. If the way we make a mess of our own lives isn't enough to convince us, then look at other people's, read a bit of history and you'll see where pig-headed conceit gets you.

"It seems to me that the Gospel says loud and clear, time and time again, 'I know you can't but I can — if you'll only let Me.' If Nina's love could turn John's life upside down, what could God's love do to ours?"

"But this all sounds a bit too close to Quietism for comfort," I said. "It almost gives the impression that all we have to do is to sit around all day like spiritual layabouts waiting for God to do everything."

"Not at all," said Peter.

"You go and tell Harry Ploughman that he's a layabout, when he's been spending weeks breaking up the ground, digging in the fertilizer and ploughing it over and over to prepare the soil for the seed. He'd probably, give you a black eye!

"If he gets a good harvest, he can be sure of two things. First, it had nothing to do with him, and second, that it had everything to do with him. In other words, the minute seed is self-contained. It nurtures within itself the inner dynamism that will produce the fine crop of oats, the field of barley, the full ear of corn. But without the labor, the toil, the spade-work of the farmer, there'd be no harvest at all."

"Now," said Peter, preparing to press the analogy home to avoid any misunderstanding, "God's love will automatically grow and develop in us like the seed. It will ultimately extend to every part of our being until it completely possesses us. And this will happen infallibly, if we will only prepare the ground, remove any obstacles required of us to facilitate the full growth of that love."

"But what is required to facilitate the growth of that love within us?"

"The answer to that is simple," Peter answered without hesitation. "By learning to pray. It's only in prayer that we come into contact with the love of God and begin to experience it entering into our lives. Nobody can experience being loved and remain the same."

"But what about me?" I said. There was a hardly detectable note of self-pity, of being "hard done by" about my question. It was the first time my question had been directly personal.

"I have known for the past twenty years that God loves me, but I've not changed. I'm just the same old me," I said with a touch of bitterness.

"Well, I don't know about that," said Peter, "but there's all the difference in the world between knowing that you are loved, and experiencing being loved. Knowledge alone is not enough. Knowledge will never change anyone decisively and permanently, but experience will, if the experience is deep enough, lasting enough."

Peter was on his feet. I hadn't noticed him getting up.

"Please excuse me, James, I simply must go," he said apologetically.

I looked at him incredulously, almost gaped with a vacant bewildered stare.

Then his words suddenly registered. They came so unexpectedly, cut across my whole line of thought. I was taken completely by surprise. Things were getting interesting. I was just beginning to talk about me!

"But of course," I stammered. I looked at my watch — it was almost four o'clock.

"Won't you have a cup of tea?" I said, in a vain attempt to detain him.

"No thanks, James," said Peter decisively. "I'm afraid I must go."

"You will come again tomorrow?" I said insistently.

"Of course," said Peter, slightly surprised at the note of anxiety in my voice. He was unaware that the matter had ever been in doubt.

I lay awake for hours that night going over the conversation and re-meeting Peter in my mind. There was certainly nothing new in what he had said. They were all the old truths but he could see them with such clarity, he could make them come alive. At least he had done that for me.

My attitude to Peter had rapidly changed. I knew he had a lot to give and I had a lot to learn. I wouldn't be going to Eriskay, or Uist for that matter. Two hours a day would be little enough time for the revision I had in mind.

4

Some people can make do with seven hours' sleep, others with six; I know several people who can manage with five. I need eight, and if I can get nine, I'll take them. That particular Monday night, I only slept for four hours.

My novice master used to quote "bed linen to altar linen, altar linen to table linen — damnation!" I couldn't imagine what fate would be in store for the renegade who could shamelessly add "...and back to bed linen again." But I could, at least I could that morning. If I wanted to rise to something more than the sub-human before Peter arrived again, I simply had to get more sleep.

When I did finally emerge, I plucked up enough courage to step outside and bid what was left of the morning a cheery "Good-day," only to discover that it, too, had had a rotten night! Disgruntled-looking clouds were scurrying across the sky, peering threateningly down as if to dare you to go more than a drenchable distance from home. I came inside and allowed myself a medicinal nip of the local wine. It is a much sought-after luxury in more equitable climates, in the Isles it is a necessity, an indispensable bulwark to fortify the spirits against the elements.

Peter arrived promptly at two o'clock. "You must be something of an oddity out here," I said, as he came in and sat down in his usual easy chair.

"How do you mean?" he said.

"Your punctuality," I answered quickly, before he could explore other unintentional interpretations of my guileless remark.

"I've always found people out here have hardly any idea of

time at all. Last time I went to Eriskay, the ferry arrived three hours late, but nobody seemed concerned."

"It's a sort of phobia with me," he said. "My father was a fanatic about time." The sheepish grin I'd observed on the first day returned.

"If he said I had to be in by ten-thirty, that meant that ten-twenty-nine and fifty-nine seconds was early, but ten-thirty and one second was late, and there'd be trouble!"

Peter smiled to himself, as he mused affectionately on the past, while he stared at the floor in front of him, gently tapping a non-existent object on the carpet with the end of his stick.

The previous morning I'd spent thinking up excuses to reduce our future meetings to two. What time had been salvaged from the wreckage of that morning, was spent trying to find excuses to extend them to five, by making use of the Saturday morning before the plane departed. I had no intention, therefore, of wasting further time with trivial ice-breakers.

I was annoyed at the way Peter's phobia about time had interrupted what was just turning out to be an absorbing conversation the day before, so I decided to carry on from where we left off.

"Just before you left yesterday, you said, 'there was all the difference in the world between knowing that you are loved and experiencing being loved,' or words to that effect," I said, eager to get things going again.

"Well, I meant just what I said," he answered, shifting from side to side, as if he had nothing further to say; but he added, "However, I do think the distinction has important implications for the spiritual life."

"In what way?" I said.

"Well…," he said, hesitating for a few moments. And then he was off.

"When I was at Strawberry Hill, I stayed with a lecturer and his wife near Twickenham Station. There were six other students and a young psychology lecturer called Mark, all staying in the same house. Mark and I found we had a lot in common and before I realized it, a deep friendship had grown up between the two of us. He was a brilliant lecturer and I often went with him to the many outside engagements that he accepted.

"Wherever he went, he would always begin by belittling his own competence, assuring his audience that he felt sure they knew far more about the subject than he did. If the contents and delivery of his material hadn't blatantly belied his preamble, you couldn't have blamed his audience if they had got up and walked out before he'd finished.

"I think it was what I originally took for genuine humility in Mark, that initially drew me to him. It was only later that I came to realize that he took a morbid delight in denigrating himself.

"It was only because we had grown close that I was able to ask him why he always had to apologize for himself, run himself down in front of others.

"'I suppose I've got what we psychologists call "a security problem,"' he said, shrugging his shoulders as if it wasn't of any consequence. 'I suppose I'm a classic case!'

"I could tell he wanted to talk, so I just kept quiet. He told me something about his childhood, about his parents, how they'd done their best for him, done everything for him that they thought was right. They loved him, there was no doubt about that. However, because of some Victorian 'hang-up' they were prepared to go to any lengths to avoid spoiling him. They shunned all manifestations of affection. He was never kissed, never caressed, never held close or cuddled, all physical expressions of love were prohibited, even though it went against the grain.

"Naturally all this came out during his training. As he looked back over his past, he could see quite clearly, without a shadow of doubt, that his parents loved him. He was absolutely convinced of it; but they'd never shown their love; he had never experienced it and that made a difference, a big, big difference to his life. Because he had not received love he found it difficult to give it to other people. He found it difficult to build up friendships, difficult to let others love him, never mind love them. That is why he felt insecure and behaved so immaturely on occasions.

"He was quite aware of his character problems and knew the reasons for them. But as he explained himself, knowledge alone is not enough. It may give you insight into yourself, but it does not give you the power to change."

"What happened to him in the end?" I asked.

"Well," said Peter, "when I went to Paris, he went to the States to do a post-graduate course. It was there that he met his future wife. I met him just before coming out here and he told me what falling in love had done for him. He said that for the first time in his life, he didn't just know, but he experienced through her love that he was lovable. He said the experience was like somebody breathing the breath of life into him for the first time. He came alive through her love and was beginning to discover a deep security, an inner strength to throw away the defense mechanisms with which he had surrounded himself over the years, and really start to become himself.

"Now," said Peter, preparing once more to press the analogy home, "...it's exactly the same with our relationship with God. Through faith we believe God loves us. We know He loves us; there can be no doubt about that. We can list all the gifts that have been showered on us to prove it, enumerate not only what He has said, but what He has actually done. But this is not enough as long as this sort of knowledge remains on the level of dry abstract truth. No matter how indisputable it is, it may be logically incontestable, even scientifically provable, but it won't deeply affect anyone.

"Knowledge alone is not enough. Knowledge alone will never change anyone permanently. But the experience of being loved will!"

Peter delivered the last phrase in a hushed, well-modulated tone of voice, then he paused for a moment's respite. He had been talking continually for over a quarter of an hour.

It was one thing to see a truth with the cold eye of an

intellectual, quite another to view the same truth with the eye of the mystic, or the poet. It's all the difference between looking at a stained glass window from the outside and looking at it from within, all aglow with vivid color, bursting with vibrant vitality and life.

Peter was able to view a truth from inside, not just because he had a facility with words, but because he was inside, himself.

For years I had identified wisdom with knowledge and sought it out with all the urgent intensity of the Alchemist in search of the "philosopher's stone." The hap-hazard plundering of dusty, mystical tomes gradually gave way to the feverish desire to lay hands on the latest theological paperbacks, as the fifties gave way to the sixties, and thrilling, exhilarating, Continental theology invaded the country.

After several years of intensive reading I emerged with a wholly new and exciting vision, only to realize with disappointment that the visionary had remained the same. If knowledge of God could not change me, what about knowledge of man, man with whom Christ had identified Himself? Surely this was what the Gospel was all about? This was the meaning of the Incarnation, that God had identified Himself in Christ with the neighbor in need. All I had to do was to discover their needs, learn how to minister to them with all the professional expertise offered by the new "salvific science of Sociology."

I became a dedicated exponent of the tenets of the Social Gospel, with all the verve and vigor of the new convert. Only somehow my practice didn't measure up to my preaching. My enthusiasm changed with the seasons, only to get snowed up in winter, where my inner reservoirs of philanthropic energy hardened and froze over. There was still a flicker of flame in my head, but no fire in my belly.

Knowledge of God had failed me; knowledge of man had failed me too.

Then it suddenly struck me like a flash of lightning; why hadn't I seen it before? The words of the Delphic Oracle rang out loud and clear in my mind. "Know thyself." Of course it was obvious! I'd been blind all along. The real problem was within me; knowledge of myself would set me free; surely this was the "philosopher's stone" for which I had been searching, it was self-knowledge.

I went away for a year to do a course in pastoral psychology and counseling. You name it, we did it! Group dynamics; sensitivity sessions; personal analysis tutorials; counseling techniques.

I know the course did me a lot of good. I got a lot out of it. My faults, my failings, my problems of character, even my personal idiosyncrasies could be explained with detailed analysis of my childhood.

At first, the experience was shattering. After the first few weeks I ended up like "Humpty Dumpty" in pieces on the floor, but bit by bit I was put together again, the better for my experience I'm sure.

At the end of the year, I felt I'd been liberated. The truth had indeed set me free. It was only gradually as the weeks went by, that I realized once more that knowledge was not enough. The psychological knowledge I'd gained about myself was true, I am quite sure about that, but it didn't give me the power to change myself. It showed me all the blemishes but it didn't help me to get rid of them. At the end of it all I was back to square one.

Peter smiled and nodded when I told him something of my odyssey in search of wisdom, as if my experience were a carbon copy of his own, which it couldn't possibly have been.

"When will we ever learn?" said Peter.

"Once upon a time, it was the educationalist who would save us; 'open a school, close a prison' was the slogan. Man's problems would be solved overnight if we could only thoroughly educate everyone. When we all had free education and the Utopia didn't arrive, they had to find another scapegoat. This time it was inflation, unemployment, housing conditions. The new religion was economics; the economists and the town planners were the saviors.

"After the war, it was science that was hailed as the liberator. It was the panacea for all man's problems, the answer to every human need. Everything was laid at the feet of the new scientific messiahs who had come to deliver man, to offer him salvation with a materialistic face.

"When people had had enough and began to prefer a human face, it was the turn of the sociologists and the psychologists; new gods, new religions, with their own hierarchies, their own priesthood and their own intolerant and insufferable brand of infallibility." Peter paused for a moment gently moving his head from side to side, his lower lip lapped tightly over the upper as he mused sadly on the tragedy of the human predicament.

"We are like stupid clucking hens," he continued, still moving his head from side to side, "...who will go any way but the right way, follow any path but the right one.

"You would wonder how generation after generation of rational animals could fail to see a truth so obvious, so simple, that even a child knows it by instinct, even before the age of reason dawns.

"We want to know fulfillment, we want to experience joy, to be lifted out of ourselves into endless ecstasy and to share our completion with others. The only drink that can slake our burning inner thirst is the living water of uncreated love. It is only under the influence of this intoxicating draft, that we will be able to see ourselves, not only as the psychiatrist sees us as we are, but as we are meant to be. It will give us the strength to grow into our true selves from the ruins that we are now. Then we will be able to reach out to the 'other' with the genuine hand of brotherhood, to give of ourselves totally in love to the neighbor in need, because we have love to give, not just dreams to share!"

Peter shifted uncomfortably in his chair, slightly self-conscious at the extravagant way he had expressed himself.

"I don't want to give you the impression that I'm anti-intellectual," he said, smiling, "or that I despise contemporary learning. Not at all. I've advised many correspondents to go on for higher studies and several to study sociology. Only a month ago, I told someone to consult a psychiatrist because I realized that they were in need of the sort of competent professional help that I was unable to give. All I want to do is to reiterate and underline that no man-made branch of learning will ever answer man's deepest needs. They may expose them, but they will never fulfill them."

"I couldn't agree with you more," I said. "I'm grateful for all that I've learned during the last fifteen or so years, though I must admit I was a bit disappointed when I found that the 'truth' doesn't set you free."

"Oh, but it does!" Peter interjected immediately. "But you are forgetting; Truth isn't just a body of facts; Truth is a Person. In God, Truth and Love are one and the same; both light and life. Truth not only shows you yourself as you are, but as you ought to be. It not only gives you vision, but also the strength to fashion that vision into reality."

Peter reached for a handkerchief, blew his nose and continued.

"To refer back to the story of Mark for a minute," he said. "His adult analysis of his childhood experience was factual and accurate and in that sense true, but his knowledge didn't liberate him because it was not The Truth. The Truth reaches out and touches the head and the heart at the same time.

"Mark's predicament was in one sense exceptional but in another sense, it is merely the predicament of all of us in bright colors. We've not all got 'king-size' chips on our shoulders, we're not all overburdened with such weighty inferiority complexes, but we've all got what he called security problems of one sort or another, we all suffer from guilt.

"In our more clear-sighted moments, we know very well that we are prize specimens of feeble human frailty. We fail time and time again to live up to even the cameo-size ideals that we set for ourselves. Day after day we experience the weakening moral incontinence that drains us dry, that leaves us apprehensive and perplexed even when we are trying our best. This is why we feel the need to hide, to clothe ourselves with layer upon layer of falsity, fatuity and fantasy, to disguise the spiritual nudity within.

"What eventually happened to Mark must happen to us, if we are to be radically changed. After all, this is what the Gospel is teaching us on almost every page. It shows us over and over again the effects of Love unlimited, as it progressively invades a human nature, the human nature of Jesus.

"It shows how under its powerful influence, He grows in 'wisdom and understanding,' as His humanity ripens and matures under the influence of love.

"To put it another way, He was absolutely sure that He had parental love. He knew by experience that His Father loved Him because that love was tangibly present to Him day after day.

"This is why He is the most mature human being that ever walked on the face of the earth. No man had ever experienced such depth or intensity of love before, nor been so absolutely sure of its continued and lasting presence. This is why He was in complete possession of Himself, totally secure, fully Himself.

"People like to present Jesus as the model for Christian action, by showing how He was so uncompromisingly available to all. They often fail to realize that He was only able to be open to all because He was first open to God. It was only because he had exposed Himself without restraint to God's Love that He was able to be filled with the fullness that He could communicate to others. Without the hidden years, the desert, the lonely garden or the inner room, there could be no compassion for the needy, no love for the loveless, no healing for the sick.

"To follow Him, doesn't mean that we should try and copy Him as an artist copies a model. It doesn't mean that we should merely imitate the outward manifestation of the inner light that burned in Him. It means that we must expose ourselves to that self-same light that it may set us afire too."

As he was finishing his last sentence, Peter reached into the top pocket of his donkey jacket and pulled out an old watch fastened to a broken strap. He put the watch back into his pocket and looked down at the floor for a moment in silence. I knew there couldn't be much time left.

There are rare moments in everybody's life when there is a sudden flash of insight that strikes like lightning so swiftly, that it defies measurement, but leaves a microscopic vision that expands in your mind like the ripples from a stone tossed into a clear pool. As the vision rapidly opens out, it loses its intensity as it spans away from the center and you are suddenly left desperately trying to hold on to the experience by hastily transposing it into words in your mind.

This had happened in an instant, as Peter had been checking his watch. Words are laborious bricks to build with, and hardly before I'd started, the vision faded into no more than a faint mirage in my mind.

When I had finished my hasty attempts at verbal reconstruction, the edifice I'd built was no more than a third-rate summary of all Peter had said, but it had been much more.

I could see how I'd been living by a string of vague ideas, parceled away at the back of my mind. Ideas I had never unwrapped fully by light of day, nor desired to, because I instinctively knew they were full of fragmentary inconsistencies, even contradictions, and they were draped with cobwebs from the past.

I'd thought myself enlightened because I'd long ago tossed aside a crude mediaeval "code mentality" that substituted law and moralism for love. I talked of love, but where I was going to conjure it from, I had no idea.

I noticed that the trendy exponents of the "conventional wisdom" became rather vague and woolly at this point, assuming as a matter of course that once the child in you had been released, then the mature adult would emerge and fountains of inner energy would flood into your conscious mind, bringing liberation, a profound inner security and moral equilibrium. "Marcus Aurelius would ride again by kind permission of modern psychiatry!"

With Peter's help I had come to realize that there is only one source of energy to revitalize man. It is only when the dynamic rays of God's inexhaustible love begin to permeate the very marrow of our innermost being that we receive the strength to stand upright and grow, to ripen and bud under its influence, and finally to open out, to blossom forth. Without this source of light, we've no more chance of growing than a drooping geranium in a dark room.

We can only begin to expose ourselves to the Light, if we are fundamentally convinced that we cannot grow without it. This is why the proud, the pompous and the pretentious will never be able to see the direction of the Light, let alone expose themselves to it. Once we see clearly that the spiritual life begins with God, everything else begins to slot into place. It does not begin first with us trying to love Him, or other people for that matter, but with trying to allow His love to burst into our lives.

If we first seek the Kingdom of God then everything else will fall into place. Only when this process gets under way properly will we be radically and fundamentally renewed, will we be able to love Him in return, create community and enter into others in a way and on a level that we'd never envisaged before. All this will be possible not just by the power of our love, but because another will live in us, and love with, and through us.

Now the way ahead seemed crystal clear, at least the central intuition of my vision remained, everything pointed in the same direction. There was now only one road for me to follow, only one way for me to go.

All I had to do, was to learn anew how to open myself to God, how to welcome His love into my life and how to experience that love throbbing within me. In short, I had to start at square one, to begin again to learn how to pray. Everything Peter had said or implied, everything I'd seen in my fleeting vision led to this same realization.

I had started years ago along the road, but been continuously side-tracked. Thank God, at last, I'd been given the grace to cry out with all the urgency and heartfelt sincerity of a prodigal son: "Lord, teach me to pray."

Peter was on his feet. There was a click as he straightened his iron caliper into a vertical position. It had been less than a minute since he looked at his watch but a lot had happened in my mind, far more than I will ever be able to tell.

"Everything points in the same direction," I said with a knowing grin, as if I'd discovered his little game.

"How do you mean?" he said, innocently unaware of what had been going on in my mind.

"Everything leads back to prayer. There is no other way forward," I said, triumphantly pronouncing an old truth with all the enthusiasm of a child who had suddenly discovered, for the first time, that two and two make four.

"But of course!" said Peter, looking at me strangely, as if I were trying to be funny.

But I wasn't trying to be funny. I'd seen something for the first time that had been staring me in the face for twenty years.

5

Next morning I wrote a postcard and ambled across to the Post Office to send it to Sheila. I had too much to say and too little time to say it. My prevailing state of spiritual euphoria prompted me to write two dramatic words on the card — "Paradise Regained!"

It was a stunning day that seemed to combine a summer's heat with a spring-like freshness. I sat by the jetty in the afternoon waiting for Peter to arrive.

After about half an hour, I could see his tiny boat making its way down the inlet from Calvay with a hardly perceptible motion. Soon I was able to hear the sound of its droning outboard, spitting and spluttering its way through the tranquil water, that looked as if it had been liberally treated with a giant-size dose of "deep dolly blue."

"Why not sit out here by the jetty?" said Peter, as he clambered clumsily out of the boat. "It really is a beautiful day."

Peter sat down opposite me and took off his heavy-looking jacket, but still left the large Aran sweater clinging to his body like a vast woolly tea-cozy. I felt hot to look at him, but I discovered he never took it off. Perhaps there was no shirt beneath, or at least no shirt clean or respectable enough for public viewing!

I told Peter what had been going on inside me during the last twenty-four hours. I couldn't explain adequately what I knew was an incommunicable experience, but I knew Peter would understand what I was trying to say. He did; he even rubbed his two great hands together in a hardly restrained expression of childlike glee and ended up by scratching the back of his head, this time with both hands simultaneously.

"If only everybody could see things in their true perspective," he said. "If they could only see what the true priorities are, they could have their Utopia almost overnight. The sad fact is, that the very people who ought to be able to point the way with a steady unwavering hand, have let the side down. It is a hard thing to say, but I'm afraid it is true. We have only been paying lip service to the importance of prayer; to the absolute priority it ought to take in our lives. That is why we have had little or no effect on the contemporary world which we are supposed to be serving.

"You see, once you admit that prayer is merely the word we use to describe the practical way we go about allowing God's love to enter into our lives to change us, and through us others, you have to admit that prayer is the most important thing in our lives. Nothing is more important than God's love, because only His love can change human beings decisively and permanently for the better. No man-made machine can do this, however sophisticated its design. No purely human power can do it, not even nuclear power.

"We might be brimming over with ideas and ideals for ourselves and for humanity, but something further is required if we are going to be more than armchair idealists. It's all very well to talk about caring for the deprived and the neglected, stamping out color prejudice, helping the Third World, creating authentic community, but it's all 'eye-wash,' it's all 'pie-in-the-sky' unless people's hearts are radically changed from within by God's love. This is the only power that can change them, and prayer is the only direct means they have of coming into contact with the power of His love." Peter paused to catch his breath. He had been speaking at a breathtaking rate of knots. He never made any attempt to cover up a slight but quite noticeable northern accent, but when he spoke rapidly and with such gusto, it became broader and broader and his language became more colloquial.

"The point I'm trying to make," Peter continued, "is that, by and large, all of us know what we ought to do in our day-to-day relationships with others. Our problem is that we don't do it. Our main problem is not with our heads, but with our hearts! It doesn't take a spiritual Einstein to name and analyze the perfect qualities that should characterize the ideal 'other-considering person,' but that won't get us very far. It's all very well to say that we ought to listen to others with genuine concern, to enter into them, to try to feel for, and with them, but how on earth do we do this? That is the question.

"Books have been written trying to analyze the model moral behavior of Christ, to put all His actions under a microscope so that we can examine in detail and in slow motion, His exemplary dealings with others; but how will this help us to do the same? They may fill us with admiration and inspire us to follow — that is their strong point, but their weak point is that they never show us how! It is the same with the lives of the saints; it is assumed as a matter of course, that the mere portrayal of heroic virtue is enough. As I said the other day, it is based on the misguided belief that if you can present perfect human behavior in an attractive enough way, you will almost compel people to screw up the necessary inner strength to follow suit and acquire the same moral qualities for themselves. The plain fact is, if people will never learn, it's impossible to compel them, at least by your own steam and with any lasting effect.

"Let me try and put it in a nut-shell," Peter said.

"Christianity is not, primarily, a moralism, it's a mysticism. It's not primarily concerned with presenting or analyzing every detail of perfect human behavior. It is primarily concerned with communicating the love that alone will enable us to be perfectly human. Once love has made us perfectly human, then perfect human behavior follows as a matter of course.

"The Gospels show us how this happened in Christ's life and promise that it will happen in ours also, if we will only allow God's love to possess us as it possessed Jesus. Our main concern is to be permeated by the love that was the mainspring of His every action; to be penetrated by the Spirit that was the source of all He said and did.

"If you want to play the part of Henry V, it is not enough to learn his lines and rehearse the gestures that you think would be appropriate to fit them. You might get away with that sort of thing in the annual school play, but you would be laughed out of court in a serious production. The role would appear for what it is — disjointed, inarticulate and contrived. Henry would appear more a caricature than a genuine character.

"If you want to play the part effectively, you must not only learn the words, you must study the man, get to know him, enter into him, let his spirit enter into yours. Then you will be able to play the part effectively because he will come alive again in you, and you will be animated by his spirit. When this takes place, you will no longer need to work out artificial gestures and movements. They will happen naturally, as if they were your own, because they will be your own.

"This is what I mean, by saying that the Gospels present us first and foremost with a mysticism; they invite us not just to copy a man who completely embodies perfect human behavior, but urge us repeatedly to enter into that man, to allow Him to enter into us, to come alive again in us and to animate us with His Spirit.

"Authentic Christian spirituality doesn't begin with a cold, calculated determination to acquire virtue after virtue, as an athlete acquires medal after medal, but with the full-blooded endeavor to facilitate the invasion of our lives by the same love that filled Jesus. When the self-same Spirit that animated every thought, word, and deed of His, begins to possess us, then the spiritual life has begun in earnest, and that same Spirit will gradually become the principle of all we say and do."

"How do we start this whole process moving?" I said suddenly. "Where do we begin?" I was like a little boy all keyed up and ready to go. Peter had been busily squirting jets of oil on the flame that he had lit within me the previous day.

"We start," said Peter, "by praying that we may be able to

realize more fully that we are completely incapable of maintaining even a semblance of true and consistent Christian behavior without the love of Christ. Unless we are transformed by Christ's Spirit, unless we are sustained and strengthened by His love, we would have a moral breakdown, our spiritual life would simply collapse."

Peter suddenly stopped, cocked his head on one side, fixed his gaze and furrowed his brow, as if he were trying to recall something relevant from the past.

"Did you ever meet Anita?" he asked.

"No!" I replied instantly, without any time for thought. I had never known anybody by that name.

"I'm only asking," he said, "because she came out here for about six months, five years ago. I just thought you might have bumped into her.

"She made no secret of the fact that she was an alcoholic, though she had been 'dry' for about five months. She was only twenty-six when I met her, but she had concertina-ed the sufferings of a lifetime into a period of about five years. She had been through two marriages and been mixed up with a seedy set of degenerates. It would take too long to go into the whole sad saga, but believe me, if they were ever to make a candid film of her life, even a contemporary film censor would have a 'field-day' with a pair of scissors, before it could be passed as screenable.

"In the end she cracked up under the strain of her lifestyle and took to the bottle. She used to get through between two and three bottles of whisky a day. In desperation she went to a local parish priest in Glasgow, but he couldn't do much for her; she was too far gone. On one occasion, he took her along to Alcoholics Anonymous in the center of the city, but she didn't want to go again, so even they couldn't help. In the end, things came to a head, when she threatened to denounce the priest to the police for sexually assaulting her, if he didn't get her more drink. This seemed to be the last straw. She had been brought up in a strict Irish home, so the way she'd behaved towards the priest shook her into the realization of how low she had sunk. She smashed every bottle she could lay her hands on and rushed off screaming for help to Alcoholics Anonymous.

"The leader of the center came out to see her while she was convalescing on the island. He told me that there was nothing they could do for anyone until they got so bad that they reached 'rock bottom' and admitted to themselves that they were alcoholics, that they were absolutely helpless. 'Then,' he said, 'we can step in and begin to help them to help themselves, but until they face reality and make this admission we can't do anything.' He admitted that one of the worst parts of his job was to wait helplessly looking on, until they reached the depths.

"He gave me a pamphlet containing the twelve steps of an alcoholic. I can't remember them all, but the first three stand out clearly in my mind.

"Number one was that they had to admit that they were powerless to help themselves, that alone their lives had become unmanageable. Number two, they had to come to believe in a power greater than their own which could restore them to sanity. And number three, they had to turn their lives over to God 'as they understood Him.' As far as I can remember, the other steps amplified these and emphasized the need for facing up honestly to their past faults and trying to make amends to those they had caused so much suffering.

"It struck me at the time, that Anita's predicament, the predicament of the alcoholic, is but a dramatic 'blown-up' picture of all of us. The fact that our perilous plight isn't so obviously dramatic is a mixed blessing. If it were, it would at least force us without undue delay to see ourselves stripped naked of all falsity and pretension, to face stark reality. Then we might come to a moment of decision that we might otherwise cowardly evade, drifting into a life of superficiality, merely existing on the surface of human experience.

"There can be no fresh start, no renewal in the life of any individual, group, or community, unless first we are able to see and admit our own inadequacy and past failures. Once we begin to see, to experience and to admit our weakness, then we can begin to appreciate the fundamental principle of the spiritual life; namely that we cannot go a single step forward without God, not a single step. The Gospel doesn't say 'without Me you won't be able to get very far,' it says 'without Me you won't get anywhere at all!' 'Without Me, nothing!'"

Peter emphasized the last word "nothing" by sweeping his hand across in front of his body with the palm flat and parallel to the ground in a decisive gesture of finality. Instead of pausing, however, to let his point sink in, he continued instantly with hardly a pause for breath.

"In fact…" he said, "let's be honest. We just don't believe this, except as a purely academic principle of theology that we scandalously disregard in our day-to-day lives. We beat our breasts with a sponge, reach for a fag and slump down in front of the telly.

"You see, if we did believe it, then we would scream out for God's help; we would go to Him; we would find time to open ourselves to His healing power; we would urgently create the space in our lives for prayer. The space and the time a person finds in their daily life is the practical sign of their sincere acceptance of their own weakness, and of their total belief in God's power; that alone will find full scope in that weakness."

"You think that the actual time we devote to prayer is very important then?" I said, knowing it to be true, but also knowing it was another of those truths with which I had but a nodding acquaintance.

"But of course!" said Peter, anxious to continue, and pleased that I'd given him the opportunity to press home something he obviously felt very strongly about.

"You might say, 'I would like to be a concert pianist, or speak fluent German, or become a scratch golfer,' but I'll only believe you mean it, when I see you practice for several hours a day. I'll take you seriously, when I see you hard at it, day after day on the piano, or swotting up a German grammar, or tramping round the golf course.

"You'd hardly meet a Christian, let alone a religious who wouldn't say they desired to come closer to God; to become possessed by Him; to build up a deeper prayer life. However, I'm not prepared to believe them, until I see them relentlessly practicing day after day, creating the space and the time to do what they have to admit is the central point of their whole lives. The desire is not enough, any more than are good intentions. Every alcoholic desires to be better, is full of good intentions, even high ideals, but something more is required.

"Learning to pray, learning to open ourselves to God, is like anything else, it needs practice and it takes time. There is no accomplishment, of any worth that I know of, that you can attain merely by desiring to have it.

"We think nothing of spending hours a day, and working for years to get a degree, pass an examination, or attain certain qualifications, and we quite rightly accept as a matter of course, that the time we give and the energy we expend is necessary. Somehow we seem to think that prayer is an exception, but believe me, it is not. Anybody who wants to get anywhere at all, in their particular accomplishment, has to give hours of time, even if they have got flair, even if they have got genius.

"I heard an interview on the radio given by Artur Rubinstein, the concert pianist, some years ago. Now here is a man who was arguably the greatest pianist of the century and yet at the age of eighty-four he admitted that he needed to practice for six hours a day. (In his prime he practiced for nine!) Though, as he explained himself, it was discovered that he had musical genius at the age of three, yet it took a lifetime to master the techniques necessary to facilitate and maintain the growth of that genius, and to enable him to share it with others on the concert platform.

"The same could be said of hundreds of great artists, performers, athletes, and people from all walks of life who reach the top of their particular branch of human achievement. What right have we to imagine that prayer is an exception to the rule, because it certainly isn't! We are supposed to be dedicated to the mastery of the 'Art of Arts' and at best we drift aimlessly along like half-baked amateurs dabbling in something that demands the full potential of the professional.

"Though we don't like to admit it, even to ourselves, we still believe that prayer suddenly happens, or never happens at all. We 'kid' ourselves that saints are born, or created, by an arbitrary decision of God who every now and then suddenly decides to 'top up' humanity's quota. This is a comforting little idea that many of us like to harbor at the back of our minds because it absolves us from serious effort.

"The truth of the matter is, all of us have the 'Spirit of Genius' within us; this is central to our belief, and that Spirit will extend His influence within us with the automatic and infallible certainty of the seed, if we only create the conditions for its growth, and this is precisely what prayer is."

"Can I try to pin you down on the point of time?" I said, interrupting Peter, because I did want to clarify what seemed to be a crucial point for both myself and for others. "Setting aside the question of content for the moment, just how much time a day do you think we ought to give to prayer?"

"That's a difficult one to answer," said Peter. He thought for a moment chewing the inside of his lower lip with his fine, well-preserved teeth.

"Take the example of a pianist," he said. "How long should they practice every day if they want to accomplish anything worthwhile? An hour a day might severely overtax them and put them off the piano for life at the beginning, but after a year or two, it might be the minimal requirement merely to keep intact what they had already learned. I'm afraid it is one of those 'it all depends' questions, that depends on the individual case. There is no general rule. But one thing I can say. If a person is only prepared to give the same daily time to prayer that would be required to reach a fairly reputable standard on the piano, then, in time, their lives will be dramatically and irrevocably changed.

"They might start with ten minutes a day and gradually extend that period as they master the preliminaries, but as the months go by, the period will gradually extend, so that in the end, the problem will be to restrain them rather than prescribe a minimum time.

"When a wholly new dimension of experience begins to unfold within them, under the influence of God's love, the ultimate question will be how to balance the hours they would like to spend in prayer with the obligations that they have to others. But believe me…," said Peter with a rather sad smile, "there are few people who have this problem."

"Do you believe," I said, "that as time goes on and prayer prospers, we ought to be able to pray for six hours a day, like Artur Rubinstein, or even nine if possible?"

"No," said Peter definitely, "I don't!" And then he added, with a twinkle in his eye, "I mean we ought to be able to pray twelve hours a day, all day in fact, and every part of it!"

He didn't wait for me to come back at him with the obvious misgivings that were leaping around in my mind.

"You see," he said, with a fading grin, "if all goes well, the prayer that starts and develops at set times, ought to spread out gradually and filter through into the rest of the day. In the end, it will become coextensive with all and everything we do. To begin with, the prayer period will be like a desert: dry, arid and barren. But it will eventually become an oasis in our lives that we cannot do without. However, that's not the end, it's only the beginning. In the end, the oasis will become a fountain that will well up and brim over to irrigate the whole of our lives.

"I don't mean that we will eventually be able to say prayers and fit in all sorts of aspirations whenever there is a breathing space in our day. I'm talking about the far more profound prayer that ultimately becomes both consistent and commensurate with intensive apostolic action. I'd rather not explain myself further now because there isn't time, and anyway I would like to explain a number of other things first. But I would like to return to this point later."

"I'm pleased you made that point," I said, "because I thought for a moment, that the ideal you were suggesting was to gradually extend the time set aside for explicit prayer, so that it would become longer and longer as we progressed, so that ideally we would be on our knees for the greater part of the day."

"Not at all!" said Peter emphatically. "If that's what God created us for, He wouldn't have made us with such bony knees. He wouldn't have needed to give us legs at all, nor arms for that matter. He could have economized all round and built us instead with fat well-upholstered bottoms to sit on, and large heads with protruding foreheads, with which to contemplate all day long.

"There is one point, however, that I would like to stress and underline and it's this: there has been a lot of rubbish, both said and written, about so-called 'contemplation in action.' The idea that we can pray in the streets, on the train, while engaged in our work, while giving ourselves to others, is absolute 'bunk' without the daily prayer of 'set times.' Of course we would all like to be free to pray wherever and whenever we like, but freedom demands discipline.

"I would like to be free to play whenever I like, and whatever I like, on the piano, but I'm not able to do so because I refused to accept the discipline that my music teacher originally tried to impose upon me. I refused to keep up my regular practice. Artur Rubinstein was only able to play what he chose, when he chose because he submitted himself to the discipline necessary to attain the full musical freedom that he desired. I might like to be free to drive Father Mac's car wherever I choose, but I can't, because I've never learned, never knuckled down to the disciplined tuition that would eventually give me the freedom that I desire.

"It is exactly the same with prayer. Of course, it is the ideal to have the facility to pray at will, no matter where we are, no matter what we are doing. But it is totally impossible unless we accept the discipline required, to learn to pray at set times and in specific circumstances. Freedom always demands discipline and prayer is no exception.

"One last point I would like to make," said Peter taking his grimy-looking watch out and studying it for a moment without any perceptible reaction. "The mere physical giving of time is obviously not enough. Many religious orders used to insist on a full sixty minutes a day at one time. It was often enjoined without any adequate explanation or preparation and approached rather like a time set aside for a salutary ascetical exercise, and usually at the worst possible time of the day.

"Beginners who may have had a serious desire for prayer initially, soon had cold water poured over their aspirations, and were put off for life, by their first hard and unwholesome experiences. As soon as they had a choice, 'prayer' was dropped. It's no good putting a child in a room for an hour a day and telling him to learn to play the piano with little music and virtually no instruction. I wonder how many musical geniuses the world has been deprived of, by stupid and callous parents who crudely tried to project their own frustrated ambitions into their children?

"One of the most shattering facts that has emerged from the hundreds of letters that I have received from all over, is that ninety-five per cent of religious and priests who write to me, have never had any adequate instruction in prayer at all."

He is right, I thought. At least as far as I'm concerned. I've never had any serious instruction in prayer and the majority of priests and religious I've spoken to on the subject, are in the same boat.

"But," said Peter, preparing to deliver a parting remark as he awkwardly dragged himself up off the ground, "believe me, there are signs everywhere to indicate that we are on the verge of a decisive breakthrough that will make Newman's 'New Spring' look like a pale autumnal afternoon; of this I'm absolutely convinced!"

An absolutely gorgeous, unaffected, childlike smile burst out all over his face; you couldn't help but respond to it, it was so infectious. I sat and watched until his boat disappeared from sight on its way back to Calvay.

Somehow it was good to be near him. I had received much more from him than words, much more than words can ever express. To be near him was to be enriched and deepened. To be near him was to be near God, that was quite evident to me now.

6

It was Thursday morn- ing already and I realized with horror that there were only two more days left. I did intend to ask Peter if he would be able to come over on the Saturday morning to see me, before I flew back to the mainland, but that might not be possible.

As usual he arrived dead on time. I did feel sorry for him, he looked so hot and bothered as he sat down in his chair. It was another scorcher outside, even hotter than yesterday, but he would persist in wearing his massive woolly pullover. At least he'd left his jacket behind. I suppose that was something.

"Would you like to take your sweater off?" I asked, half teasing.

"No, I'm fine thanks, James," said Peter, shaking his head and raising his hands, as if I were making some sort of improper suggestion. I couldn't help smiling at him. He looked for all the world like a large bewildered polar bear, that had taken a wrong turn and suddenly found himself in the tropics.

"You've convinced me of the importance of time when it comes to prayer," I burst out, before Peter could finish wiping his face with his large red handkerchief. "But now I would be most grateful if you could give me some idea of how to fill that time."

I suppose as a priest I should have felt ashamed by the spiritual nudity implicit in my question, but I wasn't. After all, who's ashamed of their nakedness when someone's handing out free clothing? Peter couldn't be deceived anyway, and who wanted to deceive him? You only feel the need to put on an act in front of other performers.

"What I mean is," I continued, to give Peter more time to finish his clean-up, "now that you've convinced me that God's love alone can change me, and that prayer is the way to expose myself to that love, could you please advise me how to start? Would you teach me how to pray, from the very beginning?"

Peter stuffed his napkin-sized handkerchief into his trouser pocket and paused for a moment, staring at the floor as if my question had confused him. Then he half laughed to himself, scratched the back of his head with his right hand and said:

"I was just thinking of the first time that question was asked and of the answer that was given. I can't do better than repeat it. 'Our Father, who art in heaven....'" Peter paused. "In the Lord's Prayer, Christ gave us the pattern of all prayer. The first two words 'Our Father' sum up the rest of the prayer and are the key to understanding the basic context and direction of all Christian prayer. Our trouble is that familiarity has anaesthetized our minds, dulled our intellects so that the depth of meaning with which these words are charged, simply passes us by.

"Take the word 'Our,'" said Peter. "This one word sums up the whole context of all prayer. You see ... prayer lifts us up out of ourselves and gradually draws us more deeply into Christ, and in Him we are drawn into the total community of mankind."

"Could you explain a little more clearly what you mean?" I asked.

"Certainly," said Peter. "I said the other day that the Gospel is the story of what happens to a man who totally exposes himself to the power of uncreated love. The Resurrection shows the inevitable consequences of this process in the life of Christ. It also makes it quite clear that what happened to Him will happen to all who are prepared to follow Him, to do what He did.

"Resurrection means that the persons who continually open themselves to love, come what may, will in the end be possessed by it. As this process reaches its climax, they will be lifted out of themselves into a new mode of being altogether. We can see this happening to Christ at the end of the Gospel story. The Resurrection pinpoints the moment in time when Christ is so possessed by love that He is raised up outside of time into a new form of existence, beyond all the laws and limitations of the space-and-time world to which we belong, and into which He was born.

"Before the Resurrection Jesus was subject to all the restrictions that bind the rest of us. He too could only be in one place at any given moment. Contact with Him therefore was necessarily limited to where He happened to be, how long He was going to stay there, how many other people wanted to see Him. Once love had lifted Him out of the world of space and time, however, He was freed from all those limiting laws and restrictions. In the eternal dimension, He could be present to countless numbers of people at any given moment, because He could be present to them, not from the outside, but from the inside, through love.

"Now He was not just the 'Man for all Seasons,' but the man for all times, for all ages, for all generations simultaneously. This is why He is sometimes called the Eternal Contemporary. And since Christ can come into contact with everyone through love, then everyone can contact each other in Him. Just as the spokes of a wheel automatically come closer to one another as they draw nearer to the center, so everyone automatically comes closer to one another as they draw nearer to Christ. The world of the eternal dimension, or the Kingdom of love, is the only place where genuine community really exists.

"When we say 'Our Father,' then, we don't just mean that we pray with Christ, and in Him, but also that we pray together with all humankind who are alive in Him, with the whole community of living or dead, because in Him there is no death. We pray with Mary too, with Peter and Paul, with Francis and Dominic; we pray with loved ones now dead, who have been reborn in Christ.

"Because prayer opens us to the world where space and time

have no meaning, our prayer can reach out and unite us with other Christians now languishing in the prisons of the world for the faith we can so easily take for granted. It can enable us to bring strength and comfort to an innocent victim of some vicious regime, who is about to be tortured at this moment."

Peter paused for a moment's respite and reached for his long red handkerchief to wipe away the perspiration that was gathering on his forehead.

"You probably saw that doctor on the television some years ago, the one who'd been tortured in a Chilean jail. She had been given electric shock treatment and been subjected to all sorts of indignities. She stated quite simply that she had received tremendous help from the prayers of friends back home. She likened their prayers to 'waves of love' that sustained her through some of the darkest moments of her ordeal. Coming from anyone else, such a phrase could all too easily have sounded like pious hyperbole. On the same news program, I heard the story of a group of Christians suffering behind the iron curtain, who had risked imprisonment to smuggle a tape recording out of the Soviet Union. The tape consisted of an impassioned appeal for prayers, from the Russian Christians to their brothers in the West. Suffering always makes people of deep faith more sensitive to the extraordinary power of prayer.

"You may be alone in your own room, or in a deserted church, but when you begin to pray you enter into the whole community of all who live and love in Christ. Through prayer we can reach out to others, share our faith and love with them, and receive their strength in return. The Church made an enclosed Carmelite nun, St. Thérèse, patroness of the Missions, to emphasize that the prayer of love transcends all boundaries, even the boundaries of space and time."

"This is what we mean by the Mystical Body of Christ," I said.

"Yes," said Peter, hesitantly. "But I always think that's rather a clumsy phrase, and it has the added disadvantage of being a religious cliché that has been emptied of meaning through over use. But the reality expressed by that traditional phrase is central to all prayer. It expresses the fundamental context in which all prayer begins, grows and is completed. All who allow themselves to be possessed by love will be swept up out of themselves, to be more deeply immersed into the life of the resurrected man, Jesus, through whom they will meet each other on a level that they never imagined possible.

"This is why the first word of the Lord's Prayer is 'OUR.' There is no place for the self-conscious 'I.' It is 'OUR' Father, who art in heaven, hallowed be Thy Name, Thy kingdom come, Thy will be done, on earth as it is in heaven. Give US this day, OUR daily bread, and forgive US OUR trespasses, as WE forgive those who trespass against US, and lead US not into temptation, but deliver US from evil.

"The whole Christian prayer tradition follows this pattern of prayer, and is exemplified perfectly in the liturgy of the Church. There is no such thing as private prayer for Christians, although they may be praying in solitary confinement.

"The context of prayer is so important both theologically and psychologically that we ought to begin prayer by mentally reminding ourselves of the all-embracing world into which we enter; of the vast community of believers with whom we are identifying ourselves, in Christ."

"I see the importance of what you are saying, Peter, from a theological point of view, but I'm not clear what you mean by saying it's psychologically important too."

"Well," said Peter, characteristically pausing for a moment. "The whole point of prayer is that it takes believers out of themselves into another world where they no longer live for themselves but for others, in a community that supersedes the barriers of space and time. They are invited into a wholly new environment where they will gradually forget their own petty self-centered world, as they learn to live with and for all who are alive in Christ.

"In other words, don't just say, 'Lord I am a sinner, help me,' say, 'Lord we are sinners, help us.' Don't just say, 'Lord, teach me to pray,' say 'Lord, teach us to pray.' And don't just say, 'Lord, I praise you!' say 'Lord, we praise you!' For you are praying with the whole body of believers who are alive in Christ and not just by yourself, and you are praying for all humankind, not just for yourself."

"I do see what you mean," I said, "but do you believe that we should never use the word 'I' and never make ourselves the subject of our prayers?"

"No, I don't," said Peter. "There are times when we have to think of ourselves, put ourselves under a microscope and even pray in the first person. I'll come back to this later, but as a general rule our prayer should place us in the brotherhood of Christ."

Peter took out his watch and looked at it in disbelief.

"Good gracious!" he said, "We have spent almost an hour talking about one word. Still, it is rather an important one."

"That leaves us one more hour for the remaining word," I said.

"So it does," said Peter with a smile, "Our FATHER." He emphasized the last word. "Yes, the first word puts us in the right context, the second points us in the right direction. You see, the Gospels show how it is the Holy Spirit who progressively invades and fires the human personality of Jesus, until He is eventually set ablaze with the love that raises Him irrevocably into the Father, to Eternity. It is the flame of the selfsame Spirit which radiates between the Father and the Son, that can reach out to us also, to fire us with the identical love that will enable all to be drawn into the community of Their life.

"Christ teaches us to call God 'Father' when we pray, because this is precisely what He is to us now. The actual word Jesus uses is even more telling than the translation to which we have become accustomed. He didn't in fact use the word that is the equivalent to our word 'Father'; instead He chose the word 'Abba.' This Aramaic word actually means 'Daddy,' or at least the word 'Daddy' is the closest we can get to the original meaning.

"Christ's use of this familiar and homely pet-name was not only new, it would have been shocking to His fellow-Jews. I don't mean that God was never referred to as Father before. Only the other day I was reading a book in which the author had actually gone to the trouble of counting the number of times God had been called Father in the Old Testament. He found there were thirteen occasions in all. However, each time the word was employed, it was used as another word for Creator. In other words, God was a Father in so far as He was responsible for His own handicraft, in the sense that we would say 'Michelangelo was the Father of his statue Moses' because he carved it, or that 'Herodotus was the Father of all History,' because he created the literary genre.

"The traditional word for Father, then, was already loaded with a meaning that Christ wished to supersede. The word 'Abba' or 'Daddy,' or its equivalent in any language can only mean one thing. What is a daddy? Who is a daddy but one who communicates life to his children. There can be no misunderstanding as to what is meant by this word.

"The nuance is crucial for the new understanding that Christ wished to convey about God. God is now no longer to be understood merely as our Father, the One who created us, but the One who chooses to share His own life with us. This one word sums up the fullness of the Gospel message: namely, that if we only allow the same Spirit of love that entered into the life of Jesus, to enter into our lives too, then we will be able to share not only in His life, but also in His action, in His love of the Father and in the Father's love of Him."

"I know what you are saying is all true," I said, "because I've studied theology for six years, but my trouble is that so often the world of faith seems far away. You've somehow made things live for me again, by the way you explain everything. But I know me, and in a few weeks everything will seem as dry as dust again, and I'll be back to the dreary desert of daily drudgery."

"This is exactly why it is so imperative that from now onwards you seriously begin to pick up the traces again and rebuild a permanent prayer life," said Peter. "By faith we know that God is Our Father, but it is only when that faith grows and ripens in prayer that we actually start to experience God's love progressively entering into us. We can call God 'Father' but what's in a word, unless that word expresses something vital and real, something that we know because we have felt it. It is not enough just to accept the bald and undeniable fact that God is a Father. If this truth is to change our lives, which it can, then it must be translated into an experience. This can only happen if we put aside the time daily, and create the space in which to allow God to become a loving Father to us. We can prevent this happening, and the truth of the matter is, we do, repeatedly.

"We just won't allow God to be a Father. We never seem to have the time. There's always something else that's more important, that simply has to be done. Until we come to realize that there is nothing more important than allowing God to be a Father, by letting Him enter our lives through prayer, then we can never be changed deeply, and will never be able to change others either. Unless we allow God to touch us with His fatherly love, we may just as well call Him Ra, Jupiter, or Zeus, for all the practical difference He will make to our lives. This is why Jesus made it clear that the one condition necessary to enter into the Kingdom of God's love, is to become as a little child, so that He can become a Father to us."

"I've never quite understood what Christ meant when He said that," I said. "We can all be sentimental about children and romanticize their innocent and simple goodness, but in reality they are self-centered greedy little mites."

"What you say is quite right," Peter agreed, "but Jesus wasn't a romantic sentimentalist when it came to children. He was aware of their shortcomings. He makes this quite clear when He castigates the Pharisees for acting like kids, squabbling with each other on the street corner. Whatever the faults of little children, they have one redeeming feature that we cannot resist. They are irresistibly helpless, and unable to manage for themselves. They have no illusions about their own strength; they are weak and incompetent and they make no bones about it. If there is anything that becomes too much for them, be it an untieable shoelace or a dribbling nose, off they run to Mummy or Daddy. They are utterly and completely dependent on their parents and they don't care who knows it. This is the characteristic that Jesus is pointing to, when He says we must become as little children if we want to enter into the Kingdom of Heaven."

"We're back to Anita again," I said.

"Exactly! Who is going to belittle themselves by getting down on their knees to pray unless they are first aware that they are in need of help? Without the basic humility of the little child, we can't even begin.

"This is why Jesus says it is as difficult for a rich man to enter into the Kingdom of God, as it is for a camel to pass through the eye of a needle. Jesus isn't just referring to the person with a fat wallet or a big bank balance; He means people who are rich in natural gifts and abilities too, the person with brains or flair, with administrative skills or business insight, with charm or artistic brilliance. None of these riches is evil in itself, far from it, but they all have the same danger. They can so easily give a person a false impression of their own strength, their own importance and personal competence. Who needs God when money will get me all I want? Who needs God's help when I can do it myself? Riches of any sort obscure this fundamental vision that all of us need to have quite clearly in mind; namely, that we are basically weak and incapable of achieving anything lasting or worthwhile without God. We are totally dependent on Him for everything. If we don't see this we're blind, and we'll stumble around for a lifetime and never find the right road, never mind enter the Kingdom."

"I must say, I'd never thought of Christ's words in that way before," I said.

Peter always seemed to be able to see that little bit deeper than me, always seemed to go to the heart of things with a simple clarity that I envied. Yet all he said seemed to revolve around a few simple truths that he kept coming back to time and time again.

Namely, the only power capable of changing a person is love, and it is the experience of the Fatherly love of God which alone will radically change a person deeply and permanently for the better. Next, a person's recognition of their own weakness is the only way they will come to feel their utter need of God's help. Third, building a life of prayer is the only logical step for the person who genuinely believes that they are completely dependent upon God. This means turning your lifestyle upside down, if needs be, to find the necessary daily time for prayer, otherwise you are just kidding yourself and will get nowhere. Prayer isn't just a luxury for priests or religious, or people who happen to have spare time on their hands, it's an absolute necessity for everyone who wants to plunge themselves effectively into the mystery of Christ's life.

"Now perhaps you can see what I mean by saying that the two words 'Our Father' not only sum up the whole of the Lord's Prayer, but actually embody the basic pattern and direction of all authentic Christian prayer."

"The word 'Our' immediately sites our prayer in the center of the Christian community, what tradition calls the Community of Saints. In this community we are all bound to each other in Christ, inextricably set in a single direction — God-wards. We are inevitably drawn into the endless ecstasy of life and love, that unceasingly surges out of the Son towards the Father, and are filled to the measure of our weakness by the Father's richness. The more we are filled with His fullness, the more we are lifted up out of ourselves in a self-forgetfulness that enables us to pray properly for the first time.

"The more we are tangibly immersed in the mystery of God's love, the more we begin to see that all prayer leads to praise, to give glory to Him, and to lose ourselves in His inexhaustible goodness. The only petition that now seems to make sense is 'Hallowed be Thy Name, Thy Kingdom come, Thy will be done on earth as it is in heaven.' From now on we begin to live for God alone. Suddenly everything else seems unimportant and trivial compared to living for Him."

"I suppose this is what the Gospel means by saying 'Seek first the Kingdom of God and everything else will be given to you,'" I said.

"That's just what I mean," said Peter. "Once a person begins to forget themselves and starts to live for God alone, then they are enveloped in the world of His Kingdom of love. Once a person is plunged into the environment of God's love, their deepest yearnings reach out towards their fulfillment, and they know that nothing less than total immersion will satisfy them completely. Once they sense and experience, in some measure, the home for which they are destined, everything else pales into insignificance. The paltry pleasures that the world calls joy, appear as dross to pure gold."

Peter was on his feet again. I looked at my watch; incredible — it was dead on four o'clock. It was hard to believe how he always knew to the minute when it was time to go. This time, he didn't even bother to consult his own bedraggled "time-piece"!

"Oh, before you go," I said hurriedly. "I was wondering if you could come over on Saturday morning for a couple of hours? The plane doesn't leave till two-thirty in the afternoon."

He paused for a moment and looked a little pensive before he said, "Yes, that'll be fine."

My heart jumped. That meant two more meetings. It ought to be enough to put me firmly on the right path.

"I don't want to be mean with my time or hospitality," said Peter, "but I'm rather 'up to my eyes' in things at the moment. I'm in the process of redecorating my cottage, and every available minute is precious."

"Why didn't you say?" I said, "I could have given you a hand."

"Oh, not at all!" said Peter. "You're supposed to be on holiday. I'm just sorry I've been unable to invite you over."

My heart missed a beat. I'd never thought that there was the remotest possibility of actually visiting Calvay and Peter's own home.

"Anyway," he said in a casual nonchalant voice that struck me "fair and square" between the eyes, "there will always be a next time."

My heart missed two more beats. I'd never thought there'd be a possibility of that either. I couldn't believe my ears. Now I knew that I'd not only discovered my own private Guru, but I'd found a friend for life!

I was so pleased that **7** Peter had agreed to come on Saturday morning, but even so there wasn't much time left, and I wanted him to give me some practical advice about what to do as I had decided to set aside time each day for prayer. As soon as Peter sat down I put it to him without any preliminaries.

Peter smiled. He had obviously anticipated my request. He reached into the top pocket of his jacket and took out what eventually turned out to be a quarto-size piece of paper, but he had so folded it that it appeared to be no bigger than an oversized postage stamp.

"I thought that would be next on the agenda," he said, grinning, "so I took the precaution of bringing along my 'Patent Blue-Print' for prayer. Quite a number of people have found it useful as a memory jog, so I asked Father James to make copies, and I send it to people like yourself. Yesterday I said that the Lord's Prayer is the pattern of all Christian prayer and that this prayer is itself summed up in the first two words, 'Our Father.' As you will see, I have translated these two words into their Latin equivalent PATER NOSTER, and used them to improvise what I think are two useful mnemonics. Perhaps you'd like to look at it briefly and then I'll explain it to you in a little more detail?"

I opened the piece of paper fully and glanced at the contents. It was headed: "A Blue-Print for Prayer": —

A BLUE-PRINT FOR PRAYER

Introduction

PRESENCE	
ADORATION	WE
THANKSGIVING	SPEAK
EXAMINATION ⎫ for PAST	TO
REPENTANCE ⎭	GOD

Middle

LEARNING	GOD
TO	SPEAKS
LISTEN	TO US

End

NEEDS	WE
OTHERS	SPEAK
SELF	TO
THANKSGIVING	GOD
EXAMINATION ⎫ for FUTURE	
RESOLUTIONS ⎭	

"Now," said Peter, after pausing for a few moments to give me time to look at his "Patent Blue-Print." "I don't like to talk about methods of prayer any more than most people, but on the other hand we are human beings, and so I believe some sort of reminder can be very helpful, especially for beginners."

"I can assure you, it will be a great help to me," I told him. Even at a cursory glance I grasped the idea, and could see that it would be a very useful skeleton.

"Before I go any further," said Peter, "perhaps I'd better explain the general idea behind the Blue-Print. I said the other day that prayer is learning to open oneself to God's love and learning how to love Him in return. Now this is all very true, but how do we start to love a person we've never really met? When we first start to pray, we feel a thousand miles away from God, and all talk of loving Him, as we understand the word love, just doesn't add up.

"However, a start has to be made, so prayer begins with the object of getting to know God, because it doesn't make sense to talk of loving someone you don't even know. The first question is, therefore, 'How do we get to know God?'"

It was quite obvious that Peter was asking a rhetorical question, so I made no attempt to answer even though he seemed to pause for a long time.

"Well," Peter continued, as if I'd admitted that I'd no idea, "how do we get to know anybody? We may play golf with them, have a game of tennis with them, we may go out for a meal, or even invite them to spend their holidays with us, but in the end we'll only get to know someone by sharing a conversation with them. We only get to know a person by talking to them, and what's more important, listening to what they've got to say. There is no other way. Getting to know God is no exception to the rule. This is why all prayer must begin by holding conversations with God, but most important of all, by listening to what He has to say. As we get to know Him more deeply, love will gradually begin to spring up and grow rapidly, but there have to be many conversations and they can be rather cold and even stereotyped initially. However, that will all change in time if we are prepared to keep at it."

"How long should these conversation sessions last?" I asked.

"I would suggest you start with a full twenty minutes each day, apart from your liturgical prayer," continued Peter. "It is imperative that you don't split this time up. Once you start to give in to yourself in this matter, you'll be down to a quarter of an hour before you know where you are, then it will be ten minutes, and you'll be back to square one in no time. Let me know how things go and I may suggest lengthening this time in six months or so. We'll see how things turn out.

"Now if you would take a look at the schema, I'll begin by explaining the introduction. The first letter is 'P.' This stands for

Presence. The first thing to do is to make an act of faith in the presence of God within you. You probably won't feel a thing, you might feel as cold as an iceberg, but that shouldn't make any difference at all. Feelings can be a great help in prayer, but they can be terribly deceptive, and they don't change reality. Whether you feel it's Christmas Day, or not, doesn't make the slightest difference to the fact that it is Christmas Day. God is present at the center of your being, the Kingdom of God is within you, whether you feel it or not. There will be moments when the realization of this presence will burst in upon you and flood your whole consciousness, but there will also be long periods when you feel absolutely nothing and you'll feel like giving up — not only prayer, but everything to do with religion. This is one of the reasons why I stress keeping rigidly to the time set aside. You see, at the best of times we are a self-centered lot and there will always be the tendency to pray when the sun is out. While the weather's fine, we'll want to pray for longer than the allotted time, but when it clouds over, we'll do our level best to pack up as soon as we can, if we haven't avoided starting in the first place."

"One of my problems," I said interrupting, "is that I get lost for words and then distractions come, and before I know what's happened, I find my mind is deluged with a thousand and one distractions from the world I've left behind, or the world I'm shortly to return to, or I slowly float away into 'cloud-cuckoo-land.'"

"Yes, I know what you mean," said Peter. "In general I would say that we ought to aim at being as simple and straightforward as possible in the words we use. Don't forget what I said yesterday. Our Lord taught us that God is Our Father, even our Dad, so there's no need to speak to Him in fancy phrases or high-sounding language. You may remember He criticized the Pharisees severely for doing this. Use your own words whenever possible and don't feel you've got to use churchy language; speak to Him as you would speak to a highly respected friend, to whom you can tell everything.

"I know this might be a little difficult for beginners, but they can always start with someone else's prayer, gradually transposing these words into their own. There are a lot of books around at the moment that can be used in this way. However, never lose sight of the ideal, which is to get rid of them as soon as possible, as soon as you are able to pray in your own language.

"One thing I think is most important to get straight from the start — you must be absolutely honest with God. Nothing short of total frankness is called for when you start to pray. Don't forget that God knows you through and through, even before you open your mouth. You might soft-soap others, but you can't fool God. If you feel like a dehydrated prune, say so; if you'd rather be sitting in front of the telly, admit it; if you'd sooner be reading a fast-moving thriller, why pretend you wouldn't? Words aren't so difficult to find in prayer if you try to speak simply, honestly, and are prepared to admit exactly how you feel from the word go.

"The next letter is 'A.' And this stands for Adoration. Although it's important to begin by realizing the closeness of God's presence, that is only one side of the coin. On the other side of the coin never forget that the One who is close to us, who inhabits the very center of our being, is the Utterly Other, the All-Holy and Transcendent God. In His presence 'every knee must bow,' we must totally prostrate ourselves before Him. Some people have found it helpful to physically prostrate themselves, since the very posture of their body helps their minds to become aware of the reality of the One who dwells within, and this in its turn enables them to find the words to express themselves more fluently.

"At the beginning of prayer I think the physical posture of the body is most important. Many people find forms of yoga help them to concentrate, while retaining a relaxed and peaceful frame of mind. All this is well and good, as long as techniques for relaxation and concentration are not identified with prayer itself. As preliminaries to create the right environment in which to pray, they are all right, but please don't think that you're missing out on something vital if you are not acquainted with Eastern forms of meditative techniques, because you're not. They can be helpful to some people, but for too many, they just become at best red-herrings and at the worst, another way of self-seeking, as they search for peaceful states of mind and experiences of higher consciousness. In other words they make what should be a means, an end in itself. Authentic prayer is always directed away from self, towards God. Genuine happiness, full human joy, is always the result of losing oneself in the love of another. Prayer is directed not towards oneself, but towards God."

"What sort of posture should we adopt in prayer then?" I asked.

"I don't want to lay down any hard and fast rules," said Peter, "but I do want to emphasize the importance of making the body work in order to keep the mind active and attentive. If you slouch over the kneeler in front of you, or snuggle into the most comfortable chair available, don't be surprised if you find yourself daydreaming or falling asleep. If you are kneeling or sitting, or using some other posture, I think it's very important to learn to keep your body in a state of disciplined relaxation, if you know what I mean. It's a bit difficult to put into words."

Peter could see that I knew what he was getting at, so he didn't labor the point, and quickly moved on to give a further explanation of his prayer outline.

"The next letter is 'T,' which stands for Thanksgiving. When I use the word 'thanksgiving' here, I am referring to what God has done and is doing for us now. For the Incarnation through which He invades the whole of creation with His Spirit; for the Resurrection of Jesus through Whom He extends His own inner life to each one of us; and for the Sacraments, by which He repeatedly renews and strengthens us in His love.

"As prayer develops, the full awareness of all that God has done grows, thanksgiving and praise merge into one, and the whole of the prayer time seems to be taken up just giving God glory for being God. This, however, is a natural development but must never be forced. When somebody gives you everything they've got, you can't stop saying thanks and why should you?

"I cannot stress too much that this Blue-Print is solely intended to help a person to love, thank and praise God. All helps to prayer are only means. They are like the boosters that lift the space ship off the ground. Once they have done this, once they have directed the point of the rocket towards its destination, they can be cast aside, they have no further function to perform. Not only can they be cast off, they must be, otherwise they will prove an unnecessary encumbrance.

"However, it usually takes time to get to know somebody so well that you just want to be with them and love them, so we usually have and need quite a lot to say to begin with. One thing that spoils most friendships before they get off the ground is selfishness, of one sort or another. It's no good swearing unfailing loyalty and love one moment and acting like a self-centered little beast the next. We have a saying: 'Actions speak louder than words,' and this applies to prayer as surely as it applies to any friendship. In other words, it's no good scrupulously setting aside a specific time each day for prayer so that we can tell God how much we love Him, when the rest of the day flatly contradicts everything we say.

"This is why the next letter, 'E,' draws our attention to the way we have attempted to love God in our daily relations with others. As St John puts it, 'If you cannot love the brother whom you see, how can you love the God whom you cannot see?' I don't want to encourage people to become morbidly introspective, but it is necessary to keep a close eye on the way we treat others and endeavor to live out the principles of Christian behavior in our daily lives."

"Do you think we should examine our conscience every time we pray?" I said, knowing that it was a habit I had lost a long time ago.

"No, not necessarily every time we pray," Peter answered. "But I don't want to minimize the importance of making honest and serious appraisals of our faults and failings regularly and trying to do something about them. The great barrier that blocks God out of our lives is, in the final analysis, our selfishness. This must ultimately be rooted out. This is a long process and can never be fully achieved without God's help, and the acceptance of the suffering that this will mean. But this is a lengthy business that will be commensurate with the whole of our lives. It is a subject that we will, of necessity, have to return to many times and in greater detail in the future. For the moment, let me just say this, unless a person makes a genuine attempt to change their lives outside of prayer, their prayer itself will never develop beyond the most rudimentary stages. Even from a psychological point of view, as you will already have discovered for yourself, if you've behaved like a prize pig all day, then prayer will be quite impossible at the end of that day. In fact one of the reasons why people run away from prayer is that they know it will mean coming to terms with themselves, and doing something about their shoddy life-style."

I couldn't help smiling at myself. Once again Peter was hitting the nail on the head, at least as far as I was concerned. He knew what I was smiling at, but he made no comment.

"'R' stands for Repentance," he continued. "I could spend the rest of the day talking about this because it's so important. Not even God can do anything for us, if we don't see how much we are in need of His help and how weak we are. The act of repentance consists of first realizing this, and then screaming out for help. The cry for help will be as loud and effective as the realization that causes it. Total possession by God will be impossible until we realize fully our own weakness and are thoroughly convinced that without Him we can do nothing, but I've already spoken to you about this the other day.

"I'm going to leave the section that I've called 'Learning to Listen' until tomorrow because it's too important to squeeze into the short time that's left this morning. I'll just go on to the final section which begins with 'Needs.'

"This is the time to recall all I said yesterday about the all-embracing context of our prayer. Not only should this be the time to pray for family and friends, but particularly for our brethren in Christ who are most in need of the help we can give; for those who are imprisoned, those who are being tortured at this moment in time, writhing in the hands of some obscene sadists; for the depressed; for the lonely; for those suffering the final ordeal alone in some anonymous death bed.

"Then we can pray for our own needs. The sad thing is that we don't even know what they are to begin with. We are so warped with selfishness that initially our prayer is not 'Thy will be done.' Even though we may use this precise phrase because we believe it's what we ought to say, deep down in our hearts we are shouting 'My will be done' and we are annoyed and disgruntled if our prayer isn't granted. It's one thing to have the right words on your lips, it's quite another to pray them with your whole heart.

"Until this happens, we just have to try our best to want the right thing and to pray that we begin to see and desire what is really good for us. Actually, one of the first signs that our attitude is gradually being changed by God, is when we begin to notice that we are starting to pray 'Thy will be done' and genuinely mean it, so that the prayer isn't qualified with half a dozen 'ifs and buts.'

"You know the sort of thing I mean: 'Lord, I wish to do your will in all things, so long as you don't ask me to give up my cushy little job, or make any major alterations in my lifestyle, and I'm sure you wouldn't want me to pack up smoking and an odd snifter now and again, and my telly is my only little pleasure, but I'm sure all these things are according to Your will, so long as they are used in moderation!'

"In other words, what I'm trying to say is that until we have been changed by God's love, our prayers of petition for ourselves will either be for downright material advantages of one sort of another, or even when we use the right words, there will be a dozen 'ifs and buts' lurking in the background of our minds."

"I see what you mean," I said, "but what you say frightens me a little."

"In what way?" said Peter, looking somewhat surprised.

"Well, I get the impression that before we can really become selfless and start asking for the right things for ourselves, we have somehow got to give up everything that we like or enjoy, as if all pleasures and comforts, even in moderation, are wrong."

"Oh dear no!" said Peter, "that wasn't the point I was trying to make at all. I was only trying to show how mixed up and divided we all are inside when we first begin to pray.

"You may remember how I strongly criticized what I called the 'tough-guy' approach to changing ourselves, because it never works. We can't change ourselves in that way. My general line of approach when it comes to self-discipline — what used to be called asceticism — is this: don't give up anything; naturally I exclude sin. Don't give up anything that you like or enjoy doing, except in so far as it stops you giving your daily time to God in prayer. But anything that consistently keeps you from your daily prayer period must go. Therefore, discipline and asceticism are not out — they're very much in, but they are primarily directed to creating the daily space and time to allow God's love to burst into our lives through prayer. Once this happens, He will progressively possess us in such a way that we will just cease to want or even desire anything but Him. What we once called our little pleasures, our innocent enjoyments, will no longer interest us any more. The same will happen to those ingrained habits that have bugged us for years; they will simply evaporate without any tortuous ascetical gymnastics. Remember what happened to my degenerate cousin, John, once love got loose in his life. When God's love gets loose in our lives the results will be even more dramatic. We have so complicated the spiritual life in the past that we have almost got to have a theology degree in order to understand it. The principal concern of the spiritual life is, how to let God's Spirit, His love, invade our lives. And it is realized by opening ourselves to His action, and closing ourselves to everything and everyone who prevents this process taking place. Prayer is simply the only way to do this.

"Oh dear, I'm getting off the point again," said Peter.

"Not at all," I replied. "What you were saying was very much to the point, at least as far as I'm concerned."

Peter looked momentarily vague and perplexed. "You were up to 'T,'" I said.

"Oh yes, so I was," said Peter, looking relieved. "'T' — Thanksgiving. Well, one thing the Gospels continually emphasize is that God didn't just create a mass of people called 'the human race,' but a community of individuals, every one of whom matters. Each one of us is a unique unrepeatable creation, 'the very hairs of our head are numbered.' God is not a second-rate workman who fashions a few spiritual aristocrats whom we call saints, and makes the rest of us working class. Every one of us is created by a love that makes us all different, and yet offers us a destiny of total fulfillment and perfection in God. No other person has ever, or will ever, possess the exact combination of gifts and opportunities that we have been given. There used to be an old song 'There'll never be another you.' Well, there won't. And there'll never be another me either," he added with a smile.

"Our trouble is, we take too much for granted," Peter continued. "We act like selfish kids who are forever whimpering about how badly done to they are. They always want what other people have got; they're never satisfied.

"That reminds me of another old song," he said, "if it doesn't sound too corny — 'We should count our blessings instead of sheep,' and when we've counted them, we can thank God for them. This is why I have put a second heading for Thanksgiving in the end part of the prayer plan, to thank God, this time for all the personal graces and blessings that we have all received.

"Now," said Peter briskly, looking at his watch, "I must move on, time is running out. 'E' stands for Examination of Conscience again, but this time, as I think I've indicated, the examination of conscience looks to the future instead of to the past. In other words, it's a time for planning the day ahead with God. Plan out the things that have to be done before your next meeting with Him. Think and pray over the various decisions that have to be made.

"On the basis of the examination in the introduction, you will be a little more aware of the moral stumbling blocks that usually trip you up. Now is the time to try and forestall them. If you have a lazy streak in you, or you've got a hot temper, or are prone to making 'smart alec' remarks at other people's expense, now is the time to take the necessary precautions against falling into these faults in the forthcoming day, and in asking for God's help.

"Use this particular time in your prayer period to look through your diary with God, not just in an endeavor to avoid the usual pitfalls that you fall into, but to approach the day boldly, to hurl yourself into it without asking too many questions."

"Without too many questions?" I said. "I'm not sure that I follow you."

"Well," said Peter, "I have a pet theory that we all think too much."

"Now I'm certain I'm not with you," I said with a smile.

"What I mean to say," said Peter, "is that in ninety-five out of a hundred moral decisions that we have to make, we know exactly what we ought to do, our problem is that we don't do it. We see the ideals fairly clearly. You don't need to be a brain of Britain to grasp that the central moral teaching of the Gospel is to love God and love your neighbor.

"The question is, what goes wrong between the moment we see what we ought to do, and the moment we don't do it? Well, my theory is, we stop and think, and then we're usually sunk, because ten to one, we'll talk ourselves out of it."

"Yes, you're right!" I said. "I do that almost every day with regard to parish visiting. If I consider going out in the afternoon, I tell myself nobody will be in. From four to five o'clock it would be pointless too, because the mothers will be collecting the children from school. If I arrived before six, they'd be in the middle of their tea, and Dad will be arriving home hungry at six-thirty, so better stay clear till eight. Everybody knows that from eight o'clock onwards the whole family will be watching telly, and I certainly wouldn't be welcome then, so why bother visiting at all?"

"That's exactly what I mean," said Peter laughing. "But what do you do about it?"

"Well, when I'm feeling in a weak mood, which is most nights, I listen to myself and stay in or perhaps visit friends. On the rare occasion I decide to do something about it I just stop listening to myself, turn off, rush out and knock on the first door before it's too late. But once I stop to listen to the well-polished excuses that are always waiting to soothe my conscience, I'm finished."

"Perfect!" said Peter. "Apply the same technique to the hundred and one other things that you know you ought to do but which you'll inevitably talk yourself out of, if you stop to think. I believe we ought to positively cultivate a habit of not thinking when it comes to certain moral actions."

"I see what you're getting at, Peter, and I take the point, but put like that, it seems a bit dangerous," I said.

"If it were made a principle for all human activity, I would agree with you," said Peter. "Of course there are moments of decision-making in everybody's life when we have to sit down and use our reason, make a list of the various 'pros' and 'cons' that will help us to make the right choice. There are borderline moral issues too, that we have to discuss and debate 'ad nauseam,' sometimes without arriving at any clear decision. All this I accept. How could I do otherwise without making a mockery of the highest faculty given to man, his reason? However, what I am trying to say is that in the vast majority of the moral actions that go to make up our daily routine, we know exactly what we ought to do, but laziness talks us out of it, wounded pride talks us into a cutting or sarcastic remark, prejudice tells us to cross over the road, or cut someone dead, the magic box beckons, we listen, we look, and are seduced! How often is the time we promised to God spent watching hours of triviality on the telly.

"Looking over the forthcoming day with God is the time to see what we ought to do and to decide to do it. Thereafter we must refuse to listen to the soothing inner voice that will inevitably lead us astray, if we stop to listen.

"This preview of the day ahead, then, is inseparably linked with making the appropriate practical resolutions that will detail the way we will hurl ourselves without question, into the task of loving our neighbor and opening ourselves up to the love of God. This is why I have ended up the Blue-Print with 'R,' for Resolutions.

"I think that's all I want to say at the moment about the plan I've given you. Please keep it and if you find it useful for yourself or for others, you can make further copies. I'll talk about the middle section tomorrow morning before you go.

"Oh, one last point that I think is very important. The Blue-Print isn't supposed to be a rigid formula. The idea is that each person can adapt it to their own needs. Some people might find it helpful to split it up so that they could use the introduction by way of a help for morning prayer and use the end as a memory jog for evening prayer, or vice versa. I know quite a lot of people who prefer to plan their day ahead at the beginning of the actual day rather than on the evening before. If you do split up the schema in this way, the middle section could be used at another time of the day as the main prayer period.

"However, absolute beginners, who are often at a loss to know how to fill their prayer period to begin with, may be well advised to make use of the whole plan so that they will find plenty to occupy themselves during the prayer period."

Peter suddenly looked perturbed as he fumbled in his pockets for his watch.

"Goodness gracious me!" he said in horror. "It's almost five o'clock, I've been deceived." He looked at me, as if I were the culprit. Then it struck me in an instant, even before I looked at my own watch. I must have forgotten to wind it up. I was right, it had stopped at ten to four.

What I had imagined to be Peter's uncanny gift of timing, was the rather more commonplace gift of good eyesight. It had enabled him to keep his eye on the time, by looking at my watch that had been staring him in the face throughout our conversations!

"I'll see you tomorrow morning," said Peter as he dashed off through the door, mumbling something to the effect that Daisy would be wondering what had happened to him. It was only later that I discovered that Daisy was his beloved and dependable cow, that expected to be milked at four-thirty sharp!

8

I awoke at about five o'clock the next morning, and although I didn't at first open my eyes, I became immediately aware of a strange atmosphere that was somehow communicated to me. I opened my eyes and sat up. The whole room was permeated by an uncanny red glow that created a sense of expectancy, as if some strange unearthly event was about to take place.

I sprang out of bed, ran over to the window and stared out in the direction of the sea. The scene that met my gaze was indescribably enchanting and will haunt me for the rest of my life. The long jagged inlet ended its landward thrust in a sharp point not more than fifty yards beneath my window. It looked like a twisted dagger of brand-new metal, polished to perfection, but it shone, not with the cold splendor of naked steel, but with the savage beauty of newly spilt blood. My eyes followed the shape of the cruel blade back to its Maker, spreading out to the horizon like a vast petrified lake, glazed with deep crimson death. The smooth motionless water mirrored its own bloody complexion upon the surrounding countryside. The sky was hidden behind thick, evenly spread clouds that acted as a perfect back-cloth, receiving the same eerie light which suffused the entire scene with varying degrees of intensity. It was as if I'd been transported back in time to some prehistoric landscape long before the primeval forests began to sprawl over the earth, before the birth of even the most elemental forms of life. I cannot tell how long I stared at the prodigious panorama laid out before me. I was so enthralled by its primitive magnificence that time no longer had any meaning.

Suddenly, I came to myself again and dressed as quickly as I could. In a flash of practical insight, the mystic was transformed into just another "snap-happy" tourist. I grabbed my camera and rushed outside.

The scene had totally changed. It was a dull, cheerless, Saturday morning, heavily overcast, with a touch of freshness in the wind that bordered on rain. Disappointed, I turned round and went inside to an early breakfast.

I don't know why, but I didn't tell Peter about my morning's adventure. I don't know why I have never told anybody about it until now. There was something intensely private about the whole experience that is wholly incommunicable.

As soon as I'd had my breakfast I packed my suitcase. I didn't want to spend time packing at the end of the morning, when I could be more profitably employed listening to Peter. He arrived at the jetty at about a quarter to ten, but he went to the Post Office first, with his old sports bag in one hand and his stick in the other. He would be sending off the week's quota of mail. It was about five past ten when he sat down once again in his usual chair.

"Now for the middle part of the schema," he said without any further ado, conscious that time was running out. "This will constitute the main body of the prayer period, and it is from here that true prayer will eventually emerge. The prayer that grows not so much from talking, but from listening. Nobody will ever be able to pray properly unless they learn to listen to God speaking to them.

"This is where most people fall down, especially beginners. At the beginning of any new friendship we usually talk too much, but as time goes on, that changes almost without our realizing it."

"I see the importance of what you are saying," I said, "but could you be more explicit in what you mean by listening to God? Does He speak to us as He spoke to Moses on Mount Sinai, or in a dream as He spoke to Joseph, or do we hear voices, like Joan of Arc?" I wasn't intending to be funny, I only wanted Peter to explain exactly what he meant, because I had been misled in the past by so much vague and woolly talk about "listening to God."

"Let me put it this way," Peter said, in no way offended by my unintentional facetiousness. "How does anybody speak to anybody else? There's nothing mysterious about human communication. We get to know someone else by listening to the words they use. Spaces between people are bridged by words. They enable us to find out more about them, they enable us to draw closer and closer, and eventually to love them. This is why the Bible has always been regarded with awe by all Christians, because it contains the words that bridge the space between God and Man: God's words. It even goes a step further by showing how God's words were eventually embodied in the flesh and blood of a man, the man Jesus Christ. When we listen to His words, we learn to listen to God; when we learn to love Him, we learn to love God. This is why all authentic Christian prayer begins not by flinging oneself into obscure transcendental states of awareness, but by trying to get to know and love Jesus Christ.

"St. Jerome said, that to be ignorant of the Scriptures is to be ignorant of Christ, and so it goes without saying that the starting point for getting to know Him is to read the Scriptures. They were written for all of us 'so that we may have life, and have it more abundantly.' They were written specifically 'for those who have not seen but who have learned to believe,' that we may come to know the 'Lord Jesus Christ and to find life through His Name.'

"When we read the Scriptures slowly and prayerfully, allowing them to sink into our hearts, then we listen to the Word of God speaking to us now. This is why whatever other methods of prayer we may at times find helpful, we must never forget, and always turn back to the Bible, as the Christian prayer book 'par excellence.'

"The early Christians knew no other. Many of them knew vast chunks of the Gospels, of the whole Bible, off by heart. They had no other prayer books to hand, nor did they have any need of them. Read Cassian's description of the way the Desert Fathers used the Scriptures, particularly the New Testament and the Psalms.

He emphasizes that they were not interested in how much they read, but how deeply they were able to penetrate the Sacred Texts. They would read a few verses at a time, going over them for a second and even a third time, poring over them, entering more profoundly into their dynamic inner meaning. The monks would pause in moments of deep silence, to allow the same Spirit who inspired the Scriptures in the first place, to inspire them also.

"When they had fully savored one particular text, they would reverently move on to another and repeat the process, leaving pauses for silence, for the word to seep into the marrow of their being. As their prayer grew more and more intense, the moments of silence would become more prolonged until in the end words would give way to a deep interior stillness. In this stillness the monk would meet his Maker in a way and on a level known only to the believer, who has given his all to the One who is the All-in-All."

"Why is it that we have lost this ancient and traditional way of using the Scriptures?" I asked. "Why haven't we been brought up to pray in this way?"

"Well," said Peter, "as you know, when Christianity spread west along the main trade routes of the world, along the famous roads built by the Romans, it found itself in what were rude and primitive surroundings, compared with the sophisticated empire into which it was born. How could you give the Scriptures to a people who could not read or write? Although it had always been the policy from the earliest days to translate the Sacred Liturgy and the Scriptures into the language of the people, how could you do this when the people had no language, or at least no written language sufficiently developed to allow such a translation to take place? By the time this became possible and people were able to read, it was reformers unacceptable to the traditional Church, who first gave the people the Word of God in their own language. This is why for centuries the Catholic Church has frowned upon, if not positively discouraged, the reading of the Scriptures.

"During the centuries when ordinary people were starved of

the Scriptures, it was the particular prerogative of the great saints and spiritual leaders to present the central mysteries of faith to the people, in a way that they could grasp. Simple devotions grew up for the illiterate, techniques of mental prayer were introduced, and methods of prayer came into vogue, culminating in the meditation manuals that we have known almost up to the present day.

"Many of these 'helps' to prayer have stood the test of time, like the Rosary and the Stations of the Cross, the Exercises of St. Ignatius, and others, but many were second-rate and have been discarded. In general these various improvisations were good because they genuinely re-presented the authentic teaching and spirit of the Gospels. In so far as they did this, and do this now, they can be used with profit.

"However, the Scriptures have been opened to all once again, so they ought to be put in pride of place. We should be only too eager to return to the most ancient and hallowed Christian prayer traditions, as practiced by all the great Fathers of the Church."

"Do you mean that the main body of prayer time should be devoted to this slow, meditative reading of the Scriptures, in a similar manner to that of those monks described by Cassian?" I asked.

"That's right," said Peter.

"I remember giving a sermon some years ago," I said. "I told people they ought to read the Bible more, and promised that it would help them to pray. The next week a member of our parish told me bluntly that it didn't work. It seemed he'd opened it at some obscure passage from Leviticus where the text went into the sordid details of how to make an acceptable blood sacrifice. He told me that it had put him off his food for a week and the Bible for life, and it certainly didn't help him to pray."

Peter laughed and said, "I always advise people to stick to the New Testament, apart from the Psalms, and one or two chapters from the Old Testament that I suggest at various times of the year. To be more precise, I usually recommend people to use St. John's

Gospel to begin with, turning to his famous discourses, especially the discourse at the Last Supper, from chapter thirteen to chapter seventeen. There's enough food for prayer there to last a lifetime. Then I suggest the letters of St. John and St. Paul, and the other Gospels."

"How do you advise people to use the text?" I asked.

"I usually advise them to use the introductory section of the 'Blue-Print' as a preparation for reading the Scriptures," said Peter. "Then to open St. John's Gospel at the discourse at the Last Supper and read some of the texts several times, pausing over them, repeating them, and asking God's help to enable them to penetrate their meaning, and to allow the impact of that meaning to burst into their consciousness. Let me show you what I mean."

Peter stopped talking, sat back in his chair, closed his eyes, remaining silent and quite motionless for a good thirty seconds before he began to speak. He began by drawing together several texts from St. John's Gospel. He repeated them slowly, unconsciously injecting into them a meaning born of long years of personal prayer.

"'No one can come to the Father except through me.' 'If you know me, you know my Father too.' 'Do you not believe that I am in the Father and the Father is in me?' '...anyone who loves me will be loved by my Father, and I shall love him and reveal myself to him.' 'Make your home in me, as I make mine in you.' 'Separated from me you have no power to do anything...'"

Peter was able to put such depth of meaning into the words that it had an almost hypnotic effect on me. Automatically I closed my own eyes and a deep stillness came over me.

He paused before repeating the texts again, more slowly this time. When he repeated them for the third time I no longer noticed the way in which he delivered them, but their meaning bore in upon me with an impact that I had never before experienced. Somehow I needed the long pause that Peter left after the final repetition to mull over the content of the texts. They had come alive for me in a new way.

Then Peter began to pray in words which were in complete accord with my own feelings.

"Lord I believe," he prayed, "help my unbelief."

Three times he made this prayer. Again he lapsed into silence. When he spoke again it was to use words of praise, thanks, and adoration. After another lengthy pause, he began to repeat individual phrases from the texts he'd initially quoted.

"Make your home in me, as I make my home in you." Then … after a short pause, "Separated from me you have no power to do anything." He repeated these two phrases several times, once again punctuated by pauses of varying lengths.

A profound recollectedness had come over me during the experience and it remained with me for the rest of the day.

When Peter had finished I said, "Thank you." There didn't seem anything else I could say, or wanted to say.

"Yes, I see what you mean now," I said, after a brief pause. My voice sounded flat and. hollow.

"The trouble is, we have got to learn to listen, to become more deeply aware," said Peter.

"We've got to learn to read too," I said.

"You're quite right," Peter agreed. "I think one of our problems is that we are bombarded with literature from all sides every day of our lives, so that we have acquired a habit of reading at a breathtaking pace, just to keep abreast of what's going on. Our only concern is to glean the relevant facts from what we are reading and to move on to something else. If we apply the same techniques to the way we read the Scriptures, then we'll get nowhere. It won't enable us to get to know Christ more deeply. We should read the Scriptures as we would read good poetry, endlessly going over it to plunder its content. People with an artistic temperament may like to use their imagination more fully in prayer, and they should be encouraged to do so. In fact everybody who finds it helpful should be encouraged to use their imagination."

"In what way do you mean?" I said.

"Well," said Peter, "you could use it to set the scene in detail before you actually start to listen to the words of Christ.

"For instance, for the short meditation we have just shared together, you might find it helpful to recreate the scene of the Last Supper in your mind. Picturing the Apostles preparing the table, seeing Our Lord coming into the room, watching Him move, looking at His face when He speaks, noting the expression. The same sort of scene-setting could be used to build up an atmosphere before you meditate on another Gospel text. The Passion of Christ, for instance, would lend itself to this method of praying. Don't just think of what Christ went through, go back in your imagination and place yourself in the event. You are amongst the soldiers at the scourging, one of the crowd during the carrying of the Cross, an onlooker at the actual Crucifixion. You see everything as it happens, you open your ears and hear what is said and then you open your own mouth and begin to pray."

"But isn't that emotional approach out of date nowadays?" I asked.

"There's no such thing as an 'out-of-date' method of prayer if it helps to recreate the genuine spirit of the Gospels, and leads a person to get to know and love Christ more deeply," said Peter emphatically. "I know a lot of people who could have made great headway with prayer if they hadn't rejected certain traditional methods of meditation because they thought they were old-fashioned. I do know what you mean though. Many fifth-rate meditation manualists, particularly in the last century, made a nonsense out of this particular approach to prayer by writing oceans of pious sentimentality that made one feel ill-at-ease in their company. Certainly this approach does not appeal to everybody, but it can be very helpful to some, and they shouldn't be put off because it's not the 'in thing.'

"The Word was made Flesh so that people of flesh and blood could understand and see God's love made tangible. Christ's death was a brutal, and painful reality through which the Word made Flesh speaks of love, in a way that is intelligible to all. To neglect the Passion as a primary source of Christian meditation and prayer is to neglect the most important manifestation of God's love that ever happened. We are not blocks, we are not stones, we are not senseless things; if we are afraid to be moved emotionally because it's not in fashion or not trendy, then we'd better start by praying for a little of the humility of the child, if we ever hope to enter into the Kingdom.

"Dear, dear," said Peter looking at his watch, "time is getting on, so I'd better make some other suggestions that would be suitable for use in the main body of the Blue-Print.

"Use the Psalms, especially the Psalms that you feel speak to you in a special way. Take them, read over them slowly, meditate on them, ruminate on them in the way I have described. Do the same with religious poems and hymns.

"There are many profound and beautiful hymns that we only glance at briefly every now and then when we sing them in church. Hymns like 'Lead, Kindly Light,' or 'Come Holy Ghost.' The hymnal can be a rich source of material for meditative prayer and I would especially recommend many of the modern folk hymns. I think the music is of varying quality, but the words are often both scriptural and profound.

"The Liturgy itself is an endless source of food for spiritual thought. An excellent way to introduce someone to meditative prayer is to encourage them to use the Eucharistic prayers. It's amazing how few people do this, but used in this way, these prayers can be of immense value.

"Use them in exactly the same way as you would use the scriptural texts. Start at the beginning, read a few sentences at a time, put them into your own words, make them your own. Repeatedly pause in silence to let the meaning penetrate. Express the way you react to them in prayer. As you exhaust one phrase, then move on to the next. Remember, there is no hurry, there's no pressure to get through them; you've got a lifetime before you.

"One of the advantages of using the Eucharistic prayers in this way is that without realizing it, you are molded into the mind and mentality of Christ's own prayer. These great liturgical prayers are the most perfected extended examples of the pattern of all prayer, the 'Our Father.'

"There are many other liturgical prayers that you can use for personal prayer. The 'Gloria,' more properly a hymn, is an excellent example. I always recommend it to people because it immediately takes them out of themselves. The focal point of the prayer is God, His Glory, and this is the end of all prayer, as of man's whole existence.

"I believe the use of the liturgical texts for private prayer is important, since it helps to build a bridge between public and private prayer. Too often they are accepted as two entirely different departments of Christian worship, when they should be seen as interdependent aspects of the believer's prayer experience."

Peter saw me looking at my watch. Time was getting on.

"Yes, we haven't much time left," he said. "All I have been trying to say is, if we would only look around, there is an abundance of material that we can use for meditation. The Scriptures should take pride of place, but there are many other sources that mirror and reproduce in different ways, the authentic spirit of the Gospel.

"To begin with, no two people will find the same methods helpful, because people are all different. This is why my Blue-Print is only designed to be an extremely flexible outline that anyone can adapt for themselves. And this is why I have briefly indicated various suggestions, knowing that many will be of no use at all, but some will."

"My big problem is," I said, "that although I may try and meditate on some of the most heady truths of the Faith, they just leave me cold, when I know they ought to be dynamite. Somehow they don't get through to me; it's as if I've built a barrier around myself."

"That is precisely the case," said Peter. "To start with, the truths of the Faith are too big, too enormous, almost too incredible for us to take in effectively. Some years ago, I listened to an astronomer talking on the radio about the more distant stars in the heavens. He said that some were over ten billion light years away. To be quite honest, he could have said a million miles away for all the practical difference it would have made to me. The distances he was talking about, the statistics he was quoting, were so vast, so tremendous, that I couldn't take them in. It's exactly the same with the truths of the Faith. Take the central truth, that God is love and that He loves me. It's just too much for anyone to take in. I can say it, I can repeat the words, but alone I cannot penetrate or comprehend the meaning. It's the same with our emotions, they can only respond to a stimulus of a certain degree of intensity.

"With good will and genuine effort all round, this state of mental paralysis gradually begins to lift. The slow, prayerful meditation on the Gospel texts suddenly begins to bear fruit. The spiritual understanding starts to stir, the emotions are touched, and begin to react. What began as rather dry academic knowledge about God changes and begins to strike you with an ever-deepening impact. Knowledge begins to turn into love, as the love that God has for us begins to register with effect. Nobody can remain the same when they come to realize that they are loved by another. We respond automatically; the emotions are released and we begin to express our love and thanks in return. This is the beginning of real prayer that will grow with depth and intensity as the truth of God's love is brought home time and time again in so many different ways, through slowly brooding over the Scriptures.

"As the impact of the Gospel message explodes with maximum effect, the believer finds that even the most extravagant words they can call upon, do not sufficiently voice the depth of feeling that they experience welling up from within. In the end the words of thanks, praise, adoration and even the language of love give way to silence, a silence that says more than the most potent man-made means of expression.

"The slow, meditative penetration of the texts, now opens out and envelops the whole being as the believer is ever more deeply absorbed into a silent contemplative gaze upon God. The most powerful and poignant expressions of the new relationship with God seem to be emptied of their meaning in the face of the reality. Words join together those who are separate from one another, but in perfect union, there is a perfect silence of bliss."

"It seems that the love of God follows the same pattern of human love," I said.

"Exactly," Peter answered. "This is why the Scriptures continually use the symbol of human love as the best possible analogy with which to describe how the love between Man and God begins and grows to perfection.

"In the beginning of human love, words are usually fairly hard to come by; there is an initial embarrassment coping with a first-time love affair. There is usually a certain strain, even an artificiality in the way in which we first express ourselves. In subsequent meetings the conversation tends to revolve around getting to know about each other in more detail, finding out about one another's background, discovering common likes and dislikes. The spark of love that was there from the beginning is fanned into a flame and words of explanation give way to the language of love. The closer love draws the two into one, the need for words grows less and less. It is enough to be together, to be alone, to be at one with each other in a profound pregnant silence."

"The Blue-Print then, is merely a suggested help to enable the beginner to build up a relationship in love with God," I said slowly, as if it had taken all this time for the penny to drop.

"That's right," said Peter, "so the moment you begin to realize and experience God's love reaching out to you in prayer, is the moment when you can put my outline in the wastepaper basket. I am exaggerating a bit. We are of course human beings; one day we find praying easy, the next we don't; one day it's Tabor and the next, it's Calvary. No, don't throw the outline away the day you find prayer easy or easier, because there will be other days when you'll be back to square one again and you'll be only too glad to return to the schema to keep you on the straight and narrow. I'm only trying to emphasize the principle, that the Blue-Print is a means and should be dropped temporarily or permanently as it leads to the reality. This is why I used the example of the space ship and the boosters earlier.

"The time will come when you start at the beginning with the letter 'P,' only to find the reality of God's love is so close and present to you that all you will want is to spend the rest of the prayer period in an all-absorbing awareness of this great mystery."

"I suppose you are talking now about the heights of contemplative prayer?" I said, in a rather reverent tone of voice.

"Good heavens, no!" said Peter, obviously surprised by what I'd said. "We've only been talking about the beginnings of prayer.

"Strictly speaking, contemplation begins not when we want, but when God wants. There will be time enough to talk about all that when the occasion arises.

"Would you believe it? It's twelve o'clock!" said Peter jumping to his feet.

"Now look, Peter, you simply must stay for lunch," I said, trying to sound as decisive as possible, so that he wouldn't be able to refuse.

"Oh dear, didn't I say?" said Peter.

"Say what?" I asked.

"Well, what I mean to say is, I'd already invited myself on the way in. I met Mrs. MacNeil and I asked if she wouldn't mind putting a couple of extra potatoes in the pot. I'm sorry, I did mean to mention it. You see, I thought if I could stay for a meal I'd be able to come to the plane to see you off."

"Oh, that's fine," I said, delighted, not only that he could stay for lunch, but that he would be coming to see me off at the airport.

Peter picked up his old sports bag that he'd left by the side of the table, and started to move towards the door.

"Where are you going now?" I said, a little puzzled. There was still half an hour to lunchtime.

"Oh dear, you will think me rude," he said. "I should have asked. I thought I would just have time for my weekly bath."

I burst out laughing. This is where I had come in, I thought, as the memory of our first meeting flashed back into my mind. Instinctively I flexed the fingers on my right hand. They were still stiff from the fearsome handshake Peter had inflicted upon me the week before. I wasn't going to be caught off my guard again, so I began to devise safety measures to avoid a similar occurrence at my departure. I would have trusted Peter with my very soul, but my right hand was quite another matter!

It was about a quarter to two by the time we arrived at the tiny air terminal.

"I'm surprised the plane hasn't arrived yet," said Peter.

"Should it be here already?"

"Well, it usually arrives at least three quarters of an hour before it's due out again," Peter replied.

Peter remained in the car while I went to check in and get rid of my large suitcase.

"The plane's been held up in Tiree for some reason or other," I said as I got back into the car. "They said it ought to be here by half-past two and will leave as soon as the pilot can be ready."

We had to wait over half an hour, during which time Peter entertained me with interesting stories about the history of Barra, going back to before the Viking occupation.

He told me how Christianity had first come to the island and how it had flourished down the ages with the help of Irish missionaries when everybody else seemed to have forgotten about them. He knew a lot about the folklore of the island too, and he had me in stitches telling me about "H.M.S. Politician." The story has already passed into legend and been immortalized in the film, "Whisky Galore" based on the book by Compton MacKenzie. The unhappy ship had been grounded off Eriskay during the last war with a cargo of whisky bound for the New World. Every seaworthy vessel for miles converged on the area! The Islanders insisted that their enthusiasm to salvage the cargo was a genuine, if not heroic attempt to refloat the grounded ship. The scepticism of the authorities was changed to incredulity when they were told every bottle had to be sacrificed to the sea in a gallant but vain attempt to save the vessel.

Eventually questions were asked about the deeper color and more distinctive taste of the domestic water supply. Questions were asked about the sudden wave of agricultural activity that induced otherwise work-shy crofters to plough unproductive land in the middle of summer!

He'd just started to tell me the story of an Islander who'd hidden his quota of whisky in the garage attached to the Police Station when there was a tremendous roar. The Island plane had arrived and thundered overhead as it passed above the car, before making its final turn over the Atlantic in preparation for touchdown. Both of us got out of the car to watch the landing and instantly had to duck almost to the ground as the plane passed no more than twenty feet over our heads before landing on the beach. Father James was first off the plane and we walked out to welcome him back. After we had chatted for a few minutes he said he was terribly sorry, he couldn't wait to see me off because he had so much to do in preparation for the Sunday morning.

I said goodbye to both of them and thanked them for everything. How could I ever thank them enough? Peter had noticed the slight hesitation I had shown before I offered my hand. He too remembered that first handshake. This time he was a little more gentle!

I had to wait over an hour before the plane took off again into brilliant sunshine. At about five hundred feet the plane banked up its left wing pointing to the sky. For a few unforgettable moments I had a clear view of Calvay from the plane window. I could see a small squat little cottage staring out to sea through two tiny windows set deep into the thick walls, proudly refusing to take any notice of the noisy modern machine that roared overhead.

To the right of the half-open door I saw Peter standing motionless, clearly definable against the bright newly whitewashed walls. His right arm, stick in hand, was raised in a last salute. Suddenly the plane straightened and I saw him no more.

Although I knew then that one day I would return I had no idea how soon that day would be. Nor did I have any idea of the strange circumstances that would lead me to live for a time in Peter's little cottage where I would discover for myself something of the spiritual journey that led him to embrace the life of a hermit in his island solitude.